More Praise for
THE LEFT BEHIND

"Wuthnow cogently confronts the question: Why are so many of the people living in small-town America filled with rage? Instead of condemning, he listens. In this highly accessible, instructive book, Wuthnow reminds readers why the so-called American Dream is closely connected to the politics of place."

> —NANCY ISENBERG, author of *White Trash:*
> *The 400-Year Untold History of Class in America*

"Analytical and humane, this account of the dense, vexed moral communities of rural America is based on profound fieldwork conducted over the course of a decade by one of our most accomplished sociologists. Conveying the anxieties and resentments that run deep in stressed but resilient small-town America, Wuthnow's appraisal of ethical sensibilities, patterns and limits of membership, and political orientations is learned, engrossing, and timely."

> —IRA KATZNELSON, author of *Fear Itself:*
> *The New Deal and the Origins of Our Time*

"Distilling an impressive body of research, this book describes the core characteristics of rural moral communities and brings important conceptualizations of rural life to audiences that may not have previously encountered them. Given the contemporary political environment, *The Left Behind* is a timely contribution."

> —COLIN JEROLMACK, New York University

"Wuthnow draws on his trove of primary source interviews and observations in small-town America, and a wealth of other materials, to effectively describe how the social fabric and moral tenors of small towns are changing. This thoughtful and effective book serves as a corrective to the caricatures of small-town America and is an important resource for our shared future."

> —COURTNEY BENDER, Columbia University

ROBERT WUTHNOW

Robert Wuthnow is the Gerhard R. Andlinger '52 Professor of Social Sciences at Princeton University. His many books include *American Misfits and the Making of Middle-Class Respectability, Small-Town America,* and *Remaking the Heartland* (all Princeton).

THE LEFT BEHIND

THE LEFT BEHIND

Decline and Rage in Small-Town America

ROBERT WUTHNOW

Princeton University Press
Princeton & Oxford

The Library of Congress has cataloged the cloth edition as follows:

Names: Wuthnow, Robert, author.
Title: The left behind : decline and rage in rural America / Robert
  Wuthnow.
Description: Princeton : Princeton University Press, [2018] |
  Includes bibliographical references and index.
Identifiers: LCCN 2017033637 | ISBN 9780691177663
  (hardcover : alk. paper)
Subjects: LCSH: Sociology, Rural—United States. | Political culture—
  United States. | Social values—United States.
Classification: LCC HT421 .W875 2018 | DDC 307.720973—dc23 LC
  record available at https://lccn.loc.gov/2017033637

British Library Cataloging-in-Publication Data is available

CONTENTS

THE LEFT BEHIND

Introduction

When the dust settled following the bitterly contentious 2016 presidential campaign, analysts scrambled to make sense of the results. One of the clearest conclusions was that rural communities voted overwhelmingly for the Republican candidate. Hardly anyone credited the rural vote with having decided the election. But the differences between rural and urban or suburban results were striking. Exit polls showed that 62 percent of the rural vote went to Donald Trump, compared with 50 percent of the suburban vote and only 35 percent of the urban vote. Further evidence demonstrated that rural voters had increasingly become Republican in each of the two previous elections. Moreover, the smaller a county's population and the farther it was from a metropolitan area, the more likely it was to have voted for Trump.[1]

The leading explanation for the growing rural-urban political divide was that rural people wanted change because they were suffering economically. A related explanation attributed the rural vote to its predominantly white population being racist and misogynist enough, particularly if resentment was involved, to prefer a white male candidate. Both explanations seemed correct on the surface. Rural areas were indeed hurting economically and they were predominantly white. Grievances about lost jobs and slurs against African Americans, Mexicans, and women surfaced repeatedly at campaign rallies. A Pew poll taken four months before the election anticipated that these would be decisive factors: seven in ten white rural residents said jobs in their communities were hard to find and white men seemed particularly bleak about their families' futures and the threats posed by immigrant labor.[2] Figures released by the U.S. Census Bureau also underscored rural hardship: nonmetropolitan incomes in 2015 rose by only 3 percent, while metropolitan incomes grew by 6 percent.[3]

Pundits suggested that the grievance-and-resentment arguments probably had merit, yet did not get to the bottom of what might be going on in rural America. Writing in the *New York Times* a week after the election, Charles M. Blow argued that rural residents were undoubtedly "suspicious of big institutions and big government [that were] located in big cities with big populations of people who don't look like them." In truth, he observed, rural communities were racially and culturally isolated while cities were cosmopolitan and diverse. In short, the divide was cultural.[4]

Kentuckian Dee Davis of the Center for Rural Strategies thought, too, that Trump's victory had more to do with culture than policy. "A lot of us in rural areas, our ears are tuned to intonation," he said. "We think people are talking down to us. What ends up happening is that we don't focus on the policy—we focus on the tones, the references, the culture."[5]

It certainly seemed plausible that the rural-urban divide was cultural. For more than a century, *New York Times* editorials had vacillated between romanticized essays about the rustic life and caustic criticisms of backward voters in rural areas who were intent on impeding urban progress. The argument fit Thomas Frank's conclusion in *What's the Matter with Kansas?* that residents in rural places like Kansas were influenced by conservative ideological beliefs to the point of voting against their own interests. The claim about a cultural divide may have also reminded readers of Barack Obama's ill-advised 2008 remark about small-town voters who "get bitter" and "cling to guns or religion or antipathy to people who aren't like them."[6]

But if the divide was cultural, was that all that needed to be said? Was it enough to suggest that rural voters were resentful because they were less cosmopolitan than people living in cities? Were rural Americans that one-dimensional? After all, some 30 million Americans live in small towns with populations of fewer than 25,000 residents. And if the "rural population" as defined in the census is tallied, the number rises to 44 or 50 million, depending on which figures are used.[7] To find out what people in these communities think—what their lives are like, what they value, and how they arrive at their opinions about political candidates and government—wouldn't it make sense to spend time talking with them?

I've spent the past decade studying and writing about rural America. It's a world I grew up in but have not lived in for many years. It's the world of politically and religiously conservative people who live in small towns, on farms, and in sparsely populated areas far from either coast. They consider their communities the heartland of America. I've visited hundreds of these communities, studied their histories, and collected information about them from surveys, election results, exit polls, censuses, business statistics, and municipal records. My research assistants and I have conducted well over a thousand in-depth qualitative interviews. We've talked to farmers, factory workers, business owners, homemakers, clergy, town managers, mayors, and community volunteers. We've listened to their stories about what they like and do not like about their communities, their struggles and accomplishments, the issues they care about, their political views, and their hopes and aspirations for their children. We've tried as best we could to set aside our disagreements with some of the things we heard, seeking instead to listen and to understand.[8]

My argument is that understanding rural America requires seeing the places in which its residents live as *moral communities*. I do not mean this in the vernacular sense of "moral" as good, right, virtuous, or principled. I mean it rather in the more specialized sense of a place to which and in which people feel an obligation to one another and to uphold the local ways of being that govern their expectations about ordinary life and support their feelings of being at home and doing the right things. This is the meaning of moral communities that we find in the writings of Émile Durkheim and in the work of many writers in his tradition.[9]

A moral community draws our attention to the fact that people interact with one another and form loyalties to one another and to the places in which their interaction takes place. These enduring interactions and the obligations and identities they entail constitute the community as a home. Understanding communities this way differs from the notion that people are independent individuals who form their opinions based strictly on their economic interests and their psychological needs. They *may be* rugged individualists. But they are not fundamentally that. Spend some time in rural America and you realize one thing: people there are community-oriented.

Contrary to the view that gained popularity during the 2016 presidential campaign, rural America is *not* a homogeneous census bloc. Nor is it a uniform polling category or even a one-party political constituency. To be sure, rural America is politically more conservative than urban America. But that fact has led to as much misunderstanding as it has up-close analysis. Arlie Russell Hochschild's *Strangers in Their Own Land: Anger and Mourning on the American Right*, for instance, is an insightful study of the resentment that led the people she studied in the Lake Charles Metropolitan Statistical Area in Louisiana, a population of more than 200,000, to support the Tea Party. But it is not a study of rural America.

Rural America is composed of small communities. Rural Americans live either in small towns or near them. Drive in nearly any direction from any city and these are the communities that dot the landscape. Of the 19,000 incorporated places in the United States, 18,000 of them have populations less than 25,000. And of these 18,000, 14,000 are located outside of an urbanized area. This is rural America.

Towns are the centerpiece of rural America. As colonists populated the Eastern Seaboard, they settled in towns. And as the population expanded along the open frontier, it established towns. Whether settlers lived in them or farmed in their vicinity, towns were essential to their survival, so essential in fact that even as the nation's population relocated to cities and suburbs, the town's place in rural America's imagination held firm.

Thorstein Veblen many years ago captured the towns' meaning in ways that still resonate with rural Americans: "The country town is one of the great American institutions; perhaps the greatest, in the sense that it has had and continues

to have a greater part than any other in shaping public sentiment and giving character to American culture."[10]

Nearly a century later, few of those who live in cities and
suburbs would think about it the way Veblen did. But many
who live in country towns would. Rural Americans realize the
nation and the culture have moved on. And yet they believe
that the heart of America still beats in small communities.

Talking to rural Americans, you learn quickly how deeply
their identity is rooted in their town. Its population may be
declining, but they care about its survival. It is where they
know people—their neighbors, the mayor, the woman at the
bank, the man at the farmers' co-op. Maybe they grew up here.
Maybe they own land. They care if the home team has a winning football season. They take pride in their community spirit.

You may not like everything about your town—there may
be a lot you don't like. And yet the town is a big part of who
you are. It is where you live, where you know people, and
where people know you. Its values rest on your shoulders and
its ways of thinking inflect your conversations. It is your way
of life. You value it and you try to protect it.

The moral outrage of rural America is a mixture of fear and
anger. The fear is that small-town ways of life are disappearing. The anger is that they are under siege. The outrage cannot
be understood apart from the loyalties that rural Americans
feel toward their communities. It stems from the fact that the
social expectations, relationships, and obligations that constitute the moral communities they take for granted and in which
they live are year by year being fundamentally fractured.

The fracturing is evident in the fact that many rural communities are declining in population. Schools are closing,
businesses are leaving, and jobs are disappearing. It is evident

in families raising children who they know will live elsewhere and in parents commuting farther to work, shop, or worship.

These alone, however, are not the reason for thinking that moral outrage is rooted in the sense that moral communities are under siege. The farm population and the population of many small towns have been declining for a century. Rural families have not only anticipated its inevitability but also encouraged their children to seek better jobs elsewhere for generations. When a moral order begins to crumble, the implications run wider and deeper. Its slide diminishes trust while bolstering protective energies. Asking "How can the problems be solved?" leads to questions about who is to blame.

Understanding the cultural dynamics presently at work in rural communities requires starting with the local norms, expectations, and habits that persons living in these communities take for granted most of the time but can readily articulate when asked to say what their communities are like. Rural communities viewed through the lens of people who live there differ from one place to the next depending on population size, history, region, and the local economy. However, there are also commonalities, including what residents laud as the desirable aspects of their communities. It matters to them that they feel safe and can enjoy the relative simplicity of small-town life. They take pride in their communities' achievements, if only something as locally significant as a new fire truck or a winning basketball team. They recognize the disadvantages of living where they do, and yet they weigh these disadvantages against the obligations they feel to their children, perhaps to aging parents, and to themselves.

Although rural communities are often surprisingly resilient, residents are keenly aware of the problems they face. The population may have edged downward for so long and so slowly that they hardly noticed, but when the school closed, that was like a blow to the gut. The closure of the only small manufacturing plant in town when its parent company relocated to Mexico did too. And so did the discovery of a meth lab in town and an accident that killed a carload of teenagers. Residents talk about these problems as if they are new or worse than ever before, even though they may not be. They worry that expensive high-tech equipment is forcing local farmers to quit. They worry that more of the community is elderly or poor and harder to assist locally. And they worry that people from other countries who speak a different language are coming in and threatening the very makeup of their community.

Faced with daunting challenges such as these, rural communities' first line of response is the people they trust and look to for help when they need it. They expect fellow citizens to take responsibility for themselves as best they can, and when they can't, for community organizations to help. Their sense of moral obligation cuts both ways: don't be a burden if you can help it, and pitch in generously when you can be of help. While some of this assistance occurs neighbor-to-neighbor, much of it is formally organized. The organization in which assistance is mobilized is usually the church. After that, the volunteer fire company, the library committee, Masons, Meals on Wheels, and a surprising number of similar organizations are present. Persons with means are expected to play leadership roles, as are local elected officials. People are proud of these traditions but acknowledge that they are not always sufficient. Like everyone else, they expect government to help.

Rural communities' views of Washington usually emerge in two competing narratives: on the one hand, the government ignores us and doesn't do anything to help with our problems, and, on the other hand, the government constantly intrudes in our lives without understanding us and thus makes our problems worse. People say they are "unhappy," "displeased," "appalled," and "outraged." The difficulty, they say, is not only that Washington is broken. It's also that in order to fix problems, you have to know the local situation (the moral order). You have to deal with people by knowing their needs and their situations, not imposing a one-size-fits-all agenda, which they figure reflects the government's urban interests more than theirs. Meanwhile, people feel the federal government is more intrusive than ever, raising taxes and imposing regulations that seem incommensurable with how things should be done.

Besides that, the moral order in rural communities includes a pragmatic, commonsense approach to local issues, which Washington seems incapable of understanding. The local community prides itself on being practical, productive, and down-to-earth even if it sometimes fails and takes iterations to get right. But community leaders recognize that the rules for engaging community problems have changed. To get anything done requires outside support, and to get outside support, you have to network and write grants. That necessitates expertise they may not have. Or it puts local affairs at the mercy of partisan state and federal politics. The frustration is deepened by the sense that Washington is all talk and no action, wasteful and impersonal, a place inhabited by highfalutin ideas and smooth rhetoric but ignorant of the common person. Residents are angry that Washington seems run by special interests that do nothing but cater to lobbyists and partisan politics. Common sense, they think, suggests that Washington has become so irresponsible, so unresponsive to grassroots ideas, that it's high time to clean house.

If the outrage in rural America is rooted in frustration that a way of life is crumbling and Washington is making things worse, that leaves for consideration the familiar argument that red state politics are driven by such hot-button issues as abortion and homosexuality. Planned Parenthood and LGBTQ advocates regard rural voters as enemies, and rural voters routinely support pro-life and anti-gay policies. The sides are indeed polarized, yet the issues are less straightforward than they seem. The evidence from talking with voters is mixed. Hot-button issues do align with Republican voting and with hopes for overturning *Roe v. Wade*, but in daily life opinions are nuanced. The nuancing reflects the compassion that may be present for a neighbor who has had an abortion or a best friend who is gay. The polarization is sharpened by organized interests that mobilize well-funded statewide campaigns that even local voters sometimes believe are serving multiple aims.

And what of the argument that "rural" essentially means "white" and "white" means bigotry toward people who are not "white"? It's true that 85–90 percent of the rural population is white Anglo. It's also true that relatively few rural communities include a substantial minority of African Americans, who, if present, continue to experience segregation, and that many rural communities are populated with growing numbers of Hispanics, who also face discrimination. These are real problems that should not be ignored. Rural residents who are African American or Hispanic describe in no uncertain terms how their lives are still affected by these patterns—how they struggle with inhumane working conditions and with threats of harassment and deportation.

White residents, in contrast, emphasize minor gains that may have been made, such as the election of a black or Hispanic candidate to the town council, but their comments betray the extent to which the "moral order" is indeed predicated on an assumption of "white-ness." Diversity for diversity's sake is rarely valued, and if it is, it means something incremental and usually symbolic. Rural communities may not be as racist or as misogynist as critics sometimes claim, but the racism and misogyny are built into the patterns of life that nearly all-white communities have come to accept. And a part of their anger is assuredly the view that the promotion of diversity is a further intrusion of big government.

Listening as people we spoke with expressed their views, it was sometimes difficult to avoid thinking that what they were saying was patently unreasonable or bigoted. My view is that the researcher's role is not to argue but to listen respectfully and thus to describe how people interpret their worlds. Within the communities in which they live, much of what rural Americans think and believe is perfectly reasonable. And, for that matter, their outlooks often express positive values and genuine concerns that any fair-minded person should be able to understand. A first measure of understanding for those who live in cities and suburbs, I believe, is to step momentarily inside these communities before articulating disagreements—and certainly before denouncing millions of our fellow citizens as hopelessly deranged.

The outrage of rural America that surprised so many observers during the 2016 presidential election was there well before, and would have been evident had anyone bothered to look. It did not happen overnight and is unlikely to diminish anytime soon. Rural voters are a minority but have a disproportionate influence in state and national politics. The rural vote needs to be understood if it is to be accurately characterized and criticized. It cannot be understood through a simple declensionist narrative about the economic grievances of rural America. While many rural communities are struggling, many others are doing just fine. The rural population may be declining as a percentage of the total U.S. population, but in absolute terms it is not. Rural residents are not leaving in droves because they'd rather live in cities. They don't, and the ones who do leave are being replaced through natural increase and immigration. Understanding the variations and central tendencies of rural voters requires spending time listening and trying to see the world through local eyes. As is true of any other segment of our nation, rural lives are complex. And to gain insights into this complexity, we must begin with a clearer view of rural communities—not as demographic categories but as the places in which people make their homes, pursue their dreams, and enact their obligations to one another. That is the basis from which to seek the sources of rural outrage and to critically assess its role in our nation's politics.

1

Communities

Among the many effects of "big data" and digitization, one of the most far-reaching is shaping the content of information itself. This is true of the most readily available information we have about rural America. National newspapers and the Internet offer a flood of facts, much of it in the form of statistics, graphs, charts, and interactive maps. This information paints a distinct picture of rural America. It is that part of the country composed of "rural areas," "rural counties," the "rural population," and "rural voters." This information is useful but it misses the most elemental fact about rural America—the fact that causes journalists, political analysts, and social scientists to call for a different kind of information that gets closer to the people who live in rural America. The missing piece is the fact that rural America is composed of small communities. Nearly everyone in rural America lives in or near a community. These are the communities they call "home."

Social scientists conceptualize homes as places in which we routinely interact with people we know and care about, places in which we conduct the most routine activities of our everyday lives and in which we feel or aspire to feel safe. Homes are places of familiarity, memory, ambience, and habit and for this reason are the spaces we can take for granted much of the time and in which we can be comfortable. This is what we mean when we say we feel "at home."

Homes can also be abusive. The rules governing them may be constraining, exercising "tyrannous control over mind and body," anthropologist Mary Douglas writes.[1] Youth frequently rebel against the rules and want nothing more than to escape. But homes are the places in which we feel an obligation to uphold the rules, if the rules are working. Homes are places that require upkeep and repair. They are places in which we expect to experience love—or, at minimum, understanding and support.

Rural communities are homes in these same respects, only more so. For most inhabitants of rural communities, the town or borough in which (or near which) they live is geographically identifiable. The town limits are clearly marked. The town not only has a name but also in most instances has a school that goes by that name, and the school has athletic teams that play on behalf of the town and the teams have a mascot. The town is sufficiently self-contained that residents do a good share of their shopping there, go to the local post office, attend worship services locally, and know their way around. The population except in the least populated communities is too large for people literally to "know everyone," but it is not uncommon for them to say that it somehow feels like they do.

That is not all. Rural communities are places of moral obligation. Residents can live there and be so independent that they rarely speak to anyone else. But if they do live that way, they are treated as outsiders. To be a community member in good standing requires speaking to a neighbor, keeping one's residence maintained, and attending some of the town's community functions. These are not the ideals of a utopian order that are seldom put into practice. They are the implicit constraints of ordinary life to which people adhere enough of the time to function as community norms.

The obligations to the community include obligations to specific people within the community. The first order of responsibility is to oneself and one's family, which in turn is an obligation to the community by taking care of one's own and not being a burden on one's neighbors. The second order of responsibility is to the extensions of one's family for which the community does provide support: the schools one's children attend, the aging relative who needs medical care or assisted living, the farm that has been in the family for three generations. And tertiary responsibilities, which are more selective, typically include community organizations and community-wide projects, such as helping with the annual homecoming parade or staffing the volunteer fire company.

The point of emphasizing these obligations is not to suggest that they are always fulfilled. Often they are not. Communities struggle, just as families do. People are too busy to pitch in. Neighbors avoid one another. Families feud. The point is rather that so much of everyday life occurs within the bounded, socially and culturally identified community that the community itself takes on the characteristics of home. Just as people identify the house in which they live as home, residents of small rural towns tend to identify the community as home. They live in such and such a place, are "from" there, and have a mental image of the place, an image sufficiently clear that they can navigate it by knowing that you turn right at the Methodist church to get to the school or turn left at the stoplight to go to the co-op. They are aware of the community's shortcomings, just as they are of their family's dysfunctions. And yet the community feels like home because it is familiar.

These are the reasons it requires understanding rural communities as collectivities, as places that people call home, to grasp why they react as emotionally as they often do when they perceive their communities to be threatened. The places they live are "moral communities" that carry meanings about the quality of life that they feel is right. The moral community influences their attitudes and how they think about the self-interests of their families. But the influence of the moral community runs deeper than that. It represents their way of life.

To better grasp the various components that constitute this sense of moral community, we need to consider what people who live in small, out-of-the-way places say about their communities. Doing so will demonstrate the extent to which people identify with their communities and how the language in which they describe these places resembles how many of us might describe our homes and our neighborhoods. In addition, the descriptions illustrate how it matters that residents have roots in the community, perceive living in small places to have genuine advantages over living in cities, and associate their communities with obligations to themselves and their neighbors.

THREE EXAMPLES

The first example is a community I'll call "Fairfield," a Midwestern town of 14,000 residents, 90 percent of whom are white Anglo and the remainder of whom are Latino or mixed race. Another 13,000 people live in a half dozen smaller towns in the county and on surrounding farms. Fairfield is located on the vast plains that stretch from Texas up through Kansas and Nebraska, the Dakotas, and into western Canada.[2]

The most noticeable feature of Fairfield is how utterly flat the terrain is. The town's grain elevators can be seen for miles in any direction. Nearly all the land surrounding it except for a ridge of low-lying hills to the north has been in crops since the 1870s, when the first white settlers plowed the prairie. Legend has it that the early settlers introduced some of the best winter wheat to the area. Today, the fields are just as likely to be growing soybeans as wheat.

The residents of Fairfield work for small businesses, in offices, or at one of several low-tech manufacturing plants, and farmers in the area grow wheat and soybeans and raise cattle. Like many small towns, the hospital and the schools are among the largest employers, but a third of Fairfield's labor force is in manufacturing, which means there are a substantial number of families who have little in common with the agricultural population, except that both worry as much about international trade as they do about domestic policies.

Compared with many small rural communities, Fairfield is a hive of activity. A century ago, the town was barely large enough to be counted as an incorporated place, but decade by decade, the population grew. An early church-related college attracted students who stayed and worked in professional jobs. Later, a junior college added to the town's white-collar ranks. Being the site of the county courthouse and also located at the intersection of two highways helped. Eighteen-wheelers now rumble through town carrying cattle and grain. On one side of town a manufacturing plant processes crude oil and natural gas, and on the other side the regional head-quarters of a national home and commercial products company provides employment. An interstate highway passes a few miles beyond another side of town. Filling stations, restaurants, used-car dealers, and a Walmart have been stretching the town in that direction for the past two decades.

Fairfield is large enough and sufficiently diverse occupationally that people mostly associate with their immediate neighbors, kin, co-workers, and people they know at churches and clubs. Nevertheless, there is a remarkable community-wide esprit de corps. Most Friday evenings from late August to late November the place to be is at Fairfield's Cougar Stadium, rooting for the championship Cougar football team. The local newspaper, which now circulates online at no charge, squeezes a few stories about state and national politics into its selections but mostly highlights the town's latest athletic achievements.

A visitor passing through Fairfield might decide to keep on going in hopes that one of the cities two hours away would have more appealing amenities. The locals, though, feel the community's size is just about right—and the ones who think it's too large live in one of the smaller villages that share the same consolidated high school. The locals we talked to said there was plenty to do, and, whatever it was, they liked the fact that it took only a few minutes to get there and were sure to have been there many times before. For one woman, it was the church she'd grown up in; for another, the Family Community Club her late mother had founded; and for yet another, attending musical performances at the high school.

Karen Meeks and her husband John live on a farm a few miles west of Fairfield. She teaches first grade in a rural school district 15 miles away, does most of the housework, helps on the farm, and tends to her mother at an assisted living facility in town. Their two-story farmhouse, surrounded by trees and farm buildings, and most of the thousand-plus acres they farm were in Karen's family for three generations. John's ancestors farmed in another community as far back as anyone can remember. The Meeks go to church in Fairfield and do all their farm business there.[3]

Ms. Meeks is the kind of rural American who puts the practicalities of living there in perspective. Living outside of town and being as busy as she is, she admits having little time to chat with the neighbors. In fact, when someone comes to visit, she often wishes they wouldn't because there's too much work to be done. The farmers she knows help each other when help is needed, but often they are too independent to ask for help. The rich and the poor in town are increasingly separated, she says. The townspeople don't want to admit that poor people are there. The population could grow, she believes, but nobody seems to want things to change. "A lot of people don't like it when people move in."

She nevertheless feels a strong affinity for Fairfield. It is her community, her home. She has lived here all her life, knows its history, and is proud that her ancestors were part of that history. She knows the fields like the back of her hand, knows where to watch when you're doing tractor work so you won't get stuck in the mud. She appreciates the natural beauty of the surrounding land, the green fields, the ripening wheat, the wildflowers in the pasture across the road. "I get a bit wispy about it," she says. And then to shift the mood, chuckles: "It keeps me grounded."

A long-term resident like Ms. Meeks sometimes envies people—her sister, for example—who have moved on and seen more of the world. The meaning Fairfield holds for her, though, is inextricably woven into her sense of who she is and why she has worth. She feels a kind of ownership about Fairfield because she knows that her family history and the town's history are joined. That history would still be hers if she lived somewhere else, but in Fairfield it is a story she can tell—has indeed told again and again—and has relatives and neighbors who have similar stories, or if they don't, still find it interesting.

The Meeks's ties to Fairfield clearly include the fact that the land they farm belongs to Karen's mother. They have considered getting out of farming several times. The work is hard and the returns are small. But her mother always put family first and Ms. Meeks feels she should do the same. She wants to be close when her mother needs her.

Others we talked to in Fairfield expressed similar sentiments about their ties to the community. The ones who lived in town spent more time with their neighbors. The ones on farms and in the surrounding villages considered Fairfield the hub of the wider community. Most of them, like the Meeks, said it took two salaries to pay the bills. That meant someone—often the wife—commuted 20 or 30 miles to a larger town for work. They had less time to visit with their neighbors and, for that matter, had more in common with the people they worked with anyway. The fabric of the community felt like home, but its edges were fraying.

A second example takes us to a town in New England I'll call Newborough. It's a fourth the size of Fairfield, which gives its residents a more intimate sense of the community. The area around Newborough was settled in the early 1700s and the town was incorporated a century later. Following an early spurt of growth, the population held steady for more than a century but has been declining in recent years after a manufacturing plant that employed four hundred people relocated. The county, of which Newborough is the county seat, has a population of approximately 30,000. That number and the population of the county's smaller villages have also been declining.

Newborough's natural beauty is its most distinctive asset. Although it suffers—as most small towns do—from too many electrical poles and overhead wires and from deteriorating shops only the locals can appreciate, the surrounding hills are balm to the spirit. The community's first settlers found it an ideal location for farming. The valley's bottomland was deep and rich, which made the soil good for wheat and corn. The hills protected the valley from the harsh New England winters. Over the years the valley's farms turned increasingly toward dairy, punctuating the landscape with tall silos and large white barns and supplying coastal cities with milk and cheese. The valley's rivers, unfortunately, also put the area at risk of floods. A few years ago, the entire valley was flooded for several weeks. Many of the farmers went out of business.

Kenneth Somers is one of the farmers who survived. Now in his fifties, he has been farming since he was a boy. He dresses the part, wearing blue jeans, plaid shirt, and a ball cap tipped back on his forehead. He and his family specialize in summer fruits and vegetables, greenhouse flowers, and baked goods. Visitors flock to the farm on weekends to sample the fresh-picked produce and fill their lungs with country air.

Mr. Somers thinks most of the people who live in the community "feel that they live in a very special place." The scenery is beautiful, he says, the history is rich with local lore, and the farms are impressive. The side roads feature two-story multi-generation farmhouses and an occasional covered bridge. The antique lampposts in town are decorated with flower baskets in the summer. The shops and gorgeous colonial houses along Main Street have been renovated to house lawyers' offices, branch banks, insurance brokers, and antique stores, all with an eye toward maintaining their New England charm. To Mr. Somers, "It very much feels like home."

It feels like home, he says, because you can walk up Main Street and have eye contact with virtually everybody you meet. You know them and that's special. Maybe it takes longer to walk to the post office because you are expected to stop and have four or five conversations along the way. But ideally you're not in too much of a hurry that you can enjoy those conversations. You can live at a slower pace. "Would I change anything? No. I like the fact that we're some distance from cities. I guess if I could change one thing, I'd want to lessen the impact the outside world has on day-to-day life here."

"I guess I need to explain what I mean by that," he adds. What he meant was that, yes, things in the valley were inevitably connected to the outside world. Travel and transportation and communication all provided the connections. And those influenced life in the valley. Still, it was what did *not* change that he appreciated most. "I look out the window at my farm right now, and apart from newer cars and trucks on the road, I could be looking out at 1910 or 1940 or 1970 or 1980." Something new might be growing in the field and somebody's house might look different, he acknowledged. But the mountain is still there. And those fields where I worked as a kid, they're still here too."

It was this sense of stability and familiarity that captured about as well as anything what a lot of people said they liked about their communities. They liked the familiar faces they saw at the post office. And yet they were also remarkably attached to the *place*. It was more than a physical location, even one as attractive as the hills around Newborough. It was a space in which lives had been lived and memories had been born— the space behind the barn where the first cigarette had been smoked, the backyard where Grandma set out a picnic lunch, or in Mr. Somers's case, the field where he worked growing up.

He's not alone in thinking this way. Nearly everyone we talked with in Newborough expressed a similar view. Some of them, like Mr. Somers, can trace their lineage in the community several generations; others are urban expatriates who've come in search of a simpler, slower, quieter life, a space that seems to have endured from one generation to the next. Besides the ambience, they like the rugged New England independence that seems more tangible than it does in larger places. They felt it was better, if they could, to rely on their own resources—helping themselves and helping their neighbors—than to rely on legislation, funding, and programs from faraway places that lacked an understanding of rural America. Sure, social services helped the community's needy, when neighbors and churches also pitched in and the assistance was tailored to be local. And, yes, the school might be small in a town like Newborough, but wasn't that better than a large, impersonal school where kids could get lost in the shuffle? What might work in cities or in populated parts of the country, people mused, was hard to imagine being applicable in rural communities.

But it's equally hard to imagine Newborough being as self-sufficient as it once was. Maybe Main Street looks charming, but older residents remember the hotel, the clothing store, the "five and dime," the newsstand, and the grocery store that are all gone. Milk prices have been so depressed that the equipment repair dealers are struggling too. The town seems deader to them than it once did. Several of the people we talked with said the community was struggling to somehow redefine itself. Change was inevitable. And, much as they hated to think about it, they knew the town would have to adapt as America continues to change.

My third example is a community I'll call Gulfdale because of its location near the Gulf of Mexico. Gulfdale is a majority-white community of approximately 3,000 people that serves as the county seat of a county of approximately 40,000 people; residents live on farms or in several unincorporated villages and work in town or commute an hour to jobs in shipyards and refineries along the coast. Compared to many towns of its size, Gulfdale has fared reasonably well. Its population has been stable since 1980. It has a community hospital, schools for elementary grades through high school, and a crowded correctional facility. The community park is well tended, the library is well staffed, and the courthouse is in excellent repair. There are more than a dozen churches and nearly as many eating establishments. Flanked with bald cypress trees, tall white pines, and rolling hills, Gulfdale exudes Southern charm—it's "right pretty," people say.

But coming into town from the south and following the bypass until it reaches Main Street, it's hard to ignore the feeling that Gulfdale has seen better days. As many of the fifties-era buildings are empty as are occupied. Except for an occasional pickup truck, the parking lots are deserted. Shuttered manufacturing plants explain why the unemployment rate is twice the national average.

"Downtown is basically the same as it was thirty years ago. There's a few facelifts on stores at the end of town, but that's about it." This is Jefferson Cahill, a portly, round-faced man in his early sixties with a spectacular head of well-groomed white hair. He could pass for Colonel Sanders if he put on glasses and grew a goatee. Mr. Cahill has operated a grocery store on the edge of town since the 1970s and for several years has served as an elected member of the town council.

Mr. Cahill says the town has remained basically the same because many of the townspeople don't like new ideas coming in and don't want it to change. In fact, they've opposed several projects that would have brought in new business. Living in Gulfdale is like going back in time, he says. Life moves at a slower pace. People like to sit on their front porches and feel safe. You can leave your doors unlocked and your windows open. You feel connected. You know the people you're doing business with. When you go to church, you see the same people week to week and year to year.

Two of the churches on Main Street have been there for more than a century. Both are doing well. One of the pastors, Reverend Simpson, says the community takes its faith in God seriously. At least the people he knows do. The annual Christmas parade is the biggest community festival of the year. He says it makes him feel better, knowing that the community can publicly celebrate Christmas this way instead of having to be politically correct about it. Each summer the community turns out for Christian gospel concerts in the park, which he also appreciates. It bothers him that God is being left out of so many other places. People in Gulfdale, he says, don't want to change the way they live. And people check up on you. They know what's going on.

"That's the way it is in a community like this. It's not a bad thing. It keeps you from doing something stupid. It keeps you from venturing off into something you're not supposed to. It keeps things balanced."

Balanced? Like most small towns, words have local meanings that take a while to understand. In Gulfdale, "balanced" means a couple of things. It connotes being well-mannered and temperate, Southern white middle-class style, unlike the crude, reckless behavior one might find among "certain elements" and at the shipyards. "Balanced" also serves as a euphemism for the community's power structure, which maintains a kind of stalemate that prevents, say, the construction industry or the utilities company from gaining the upper hand. When people in Gulfdale declare they want things to stay as they are, they sometimes mean only that things could get worse.

Whether they like it or not, though, Gulfdale is changing. The stores don't close on Saturday afternoons like they used to. They're now open on Sundays too. There was a ban on liquor in the county since 1920. The citizens finally repealed it in a recent referendum. Newer families in the community seem to be coming from a different culture. They don't seem to fit in, old-timers say. It's hard to know if they ever will.

Serving on the town council, as he does, Mr. Cahill has made it his business to talk with people in different parts of the community and listen to their concerns. Race relations? Yes, the community was making progress. Jobs? Well, the unemployment rate was high, but the fifth of the population that was suffering the most was "getting some type of supplement." He isn't sure they deserve it, but that isn't the community's biggest worry.

The biggest problem, he says, was that federal law had resulted in a fifty-unit federal housing project being built in Gulfdale five or six years ago. And that was more than enough! "You just get the wrong element in a housing project like that where everybody gets subsidized rent." There was one situation, he says, where at least fourteen people must have been living in the same unit. "It's just hard to keep the bad element out."

Fortunately for the community's white middle-class majority, the federal housing project was at the opposite corner of town from most of the upscale residences. For that part of the community, Gulfdale was mostly a pleasant place to live. A recent zoning ordinance had gone into effect to keep the trailer park where it was supposed to be. The three largest churches in town were each doing well, and even though they rarely cooperated on anything, they did keep the Christmas festival and the summer gospel concerts in business.

Whether it was fear of the "wrong element" or a more generous spirit of being loosely united as Christians, the people we spoke with in Gulfdale did register a strong affinity for their community. They appreciated feeling in control of their lives, which they asserted would not be true in a city. They enjoyed meeting friends and neighbors for coffee, coming away feeling they shared common values, and knowing that if they didn't, the polite thing was not to talk about them, especially if politics were at issue. Above all, they prided themselves on knowing what Southern hospitality meant and putting it into practice. It meant knowing that people would wave at you and greet you when they didn't even know you. It meant responding in kind. It wasn't strange to do that in Gulfdale. It was simply a way of saying "we appreciate you; you're important."

A PLACE CALLED HOME

I doubt that many of the details in these examples are surprising. Whether we live in cities and suburbs or in small towns, the popular stereotypes of rural places are familiar: slow-paced, friendly, stuck in the past, resistant to change. But we need to push these characteristics to see what they mean and why they are important. Why does seeing people on the way to the post office matter? Why is it good for people to know what you're doing? Stereotypes usually convey some truth. These are no exception.

The place to begin is people's perception in rural communities that the community feels like home. The reason is plausibly that they have lived there a long time. An indication of this possibility is that the median age of adults (eighteen years and over) in rural counties is six years older than in urban counties—fifty-one versus forty-five.[4] A further indication is survey evidence showing that 80 percent of rural residents were raised in a small town or rural area (although not necessarily the one in which they currently live).[5]

Another contributing factor is that people in predominantly rural states are more likely to remain in their state of origin than people in urban states. This is particularly true of rural people who do not graduate from college, of whom there is a higher percentage than in cities. Among college graduates in nonmetropolitan communities, 37 percent already live outside their birth state by the time they graduate, and this proportion rises steadily until 45 percent do by the time they are forty. The pattern among those who do not graduate from college is different. Thirty percent live outside their birth state at age twenty-three and the proportion rises only to 33 percent over the next decade, then remains at 33 percent. They don't necessarily stay in the same community, but the pattern suggests a lack of geographic mobility.

Why they so often stay is complicated. Some are tethered to farms, small businesses, and relatives. Some left and came back, perhaps having failed to fit in somewhere else. Others never considered leaving. The ones who stayed by no means felt the grass was necessarily greener on their side of the fence. Some of them admitted it was a spouse or parent who anchored them in place. For the most part, though, they had not only made peace with where they were but found ample reasons to say they wanted to stay.

They liked the familiarity of living in a small community. Traffic was minimal. They could walk to the store or drive there in a few minutes. It wasn't only that you could get there quickly; you also knew where everything was and could get there without thinking. You knew how to communicate, too, because you knew the local slang. For instance, what's a roscoe? People in one community might know and others wouldn't. There was even a marked somatic disposition toward familiar sights and smells, as one man remarked about the fresh-mown hay near where he lives outside of Fairfield, and as a woman in Gulfdale explained in saying she can breathe better in her rural community than she can in a city.

The longer a person lives somewhere, the more likely it is to feel like home. However, there is a second, subtler dynamic at work in rural communities. Many of the people who lived in their communities for less than two decades said they still didn't feel like they quite belonged. Small towns are not exactly gerontocracies. But it can feel like they are. The old-timers set the norms that newcomers feel compelled to accept if they want to fit in. This is one of the reasons the norms seem to change so slowly. Inertia takes hold. What seems right is what has seemed right for a long time.

How are the norms communicated? This is part of what happens when people have conversations on the way to the post office. It happens when they greet the same people at church year after year and attend school functions or farm bureau meetings. Suppose the conversation at the post office goes like this: "I was talking to Mildred at the co-op the other day and she said your daughter is getting married!" You don't know Mildred that well, so maybe you are mildly surprised. But you live in a small town, so you aren't *that* surprised. The encounter reminds you that the people you know in town know other people in town and they talk about you and your family when you aren't present. It's not just confirmation that gossip prevails in small towns. It's also evidence that your life is on display even when you think it may not be. If you care about fitting in, it matters what you do and say.

Here is another example. You're walking to the post office and you meet someone you don't know. But you still know what to do. If they are dressed a certain way and act a certain way, you know they are from out of town. You don't look them right in the eye but you ask someone at the post office who the stranger is. If they look at you *as if* they know you, you also must act *as if* you know them. You know whether the appropriate response in your community is "mornin'," "hey," "nice out today, isn't it," or something else. Similarly, you know when you meet someone while driving whether the appropriate wave is arm out the window, full-hand wave from inside your vehicle, two-fingered palm-on-steering-wheel salute, horn honk, or none of the above.

The conversation in which you learn that Mildred knows your daughter is getting married points to a more serious aspect of rural community etiquette. The appropriate response if a date for the wedding has been set is to tell your interlocutor how pleased you would be if they could come. And your interlocutor's response should be, yes, I'd like that, and is there anything I can do to help? An interaction of this kind is in small but important measure an indication of the way living in a rural community entails moral obligations. Perhaps there are mitigating circumstances such as going to a different church or being part of a different extended kin network that prevent you from having to offer or accept help with the wedding. If your neighbor is in the hospital, no such mitigating circumstances exist. Being a good neighbor means going to visit and offering to help take in the mail or bring over a covered dish. If your neighbor is a farmer, you and the other neighbors are expected to help do the chores and finish cutting the corn.

KNOWING EVERYONE

Two of the commonest statements you hear in rural communities are "everybody knows everybody else here" and "we're all pretty much the same here." A moment's reflection shows that neither statement can be literally true. In a town of only 1,000 people, you aren't likely to know them all, and if you did, that would be far more than most people claim to have met in other contexts or have "friended" on Facebook. "All the same" defies logic as well. People in small places vary in interests, occupations, and lifestyles just as they do elsewhere.

How people can plausibly claim to know everyone in town stems from two of the norms I've already mentioned. One is that you and the person you do not know when you meet on the sidewalk act *as if* you do, which leaves you thinking perhaps you do know each other, or if not, at least you both know the code for acting as if you do ("speak to them anyway," a long-time Newborough resident explained). The other is Mildred at the co-op. You don't know Mildred, but you've just learned that she knows your daughter is getting married, so in that case perhaps she knows enough about you that you should consider her someone you know.

The sense of knowing everyone is thus a statement about being part of a community, not a literal estimate of the size of your social network. With slight modification, what anthropologist Benedict Anderson famously observed of nations pertains equally to rural towns. Community is *imagined*, Anderson says, "Because the members of even the smallest [ones] will never know [all] of their fellow-members, meet them, or even hear of them, yet in the minds of each lives the image of their communion."[6]

Even though everyone literally does not know everyone else, the chances of any two people in a small community knowing each other are also higher than in a larger place. Residents who went to school in the town and still live there are likely to know each other from childhood. Rural residents are often members of extended and intermarried families who live in the same community. It matters, too, to get to know people if you want to have good business relationships with them. The local norm is to expect better treatment at the bank if you chat for a few minutes with the clerk. The same is true of the person who fixes your washing machine. That person is likely to be the person you call next time an appliance breaks.

This is not only the way to get things done but also the reason to be polite. An office worker in Newborough explained it well when she said what it means to be in a place where you keep seeing the same people year after year. "You don't want to offend them. So even if you disagree, you let it go. You're going to see them in your daily business and at every community event. Unless it's important, you're not going to push it."

The statement that residents in small communities are the same is clearly untrue if standard measures of income diversity are considered. The probability of any two households falling into the same income bracket is marginally higher in towns of 25,000 people or less than in larger towns. Only the smallest towns with fewer than 1,000 people are the true outliers, though. Diversity is even relatively more similar in small towns and cities by another measure. When interviewers conducting a national in-household survey were asked to rank interviewees' homes on a "far above average" to "far below average" scale, the rankings were nearly the same in small towns, suburbs, and cities. And if interviewers' rankings resembled the same evidence people in these communities took account of day by day, it meant that residents were aware of how much homes in their communities varied. To be sure, few multimillionaires live in small towns. Yet the top 1 percent in towns under 25,000 people earn five times the median amount on average, while approximately 25 percent of households have incomes less than half the median amount.[7]

The most visible differences in local contexts are the jobs people hold and the lifestyles associated with these jobs. In the towns I studied, people grouped themselves and their neighbors into several broad categories. At the top are the "gentry" who farm or manage large farms, own large land-holdings or businesses, or hold high-paying jobs as doctors or lawyers. Their townspeople consider them wealthy and they live in expensive houses, take expensive vacations, and belong to the country club, if there is one, and in many instances, own a boat or a vacation home. Fewer than 5 percent of the families in most communities fall into this category.

The "service class" is next in terms of prestige in the community and lifestyles. They are employees who work as accountants, bank managers, teachers, registered nurses, administrators, and government officials. Approximately 20 percent of the civilian labor force in rural communities are employed as teachers, school administrators, and in the various health professions. Another 15 percent work in various public administration, financial administration, and insurance jobs. They are usually more mobile than the gentry, whose land and businesses keep them in place. They live in small towns by choice often because of family connections or an affinity for the region.

"Wageworkers" make up a third category. Unlike the service class, they rarely have attended college. They work in meat-processing plants, oil refineries, mines, and pipeline stations, at feedlots and on truck farms, in construction, and as waitresses, telemarketers, insurance claims processors, teaching assistants, nursing aides, cooks, school bus drivers, and custodians. Approximately 15 percent of the civilian labor force in these towns work in manufacturing, 8 percent in construction, 6 percent in trucking and delivery, and another 15 percent or so in retail stores and offices.

"Pensioners" are a fourth category. They make up approximately 20 percent of the population in rural communities.

They are retired or semi-retired and live on often-meager retirement income, investments, pensions, and Social Security. Many have children or grandchildren in the area who provide aid and in some cases, financial help. Many live in low-income housing designated for senior citizens or in assisted living facilities and nursing homes. The smaller the community, the larger the proportion of population who are age sixty-five and older.

In addition to the foregoing, 10–20 percent of residents in rural communities live below the poverty line. They include wageworkers earning less than the minimum wage, temporarily unemployed, or doing seasonal work; the elderly; persons with disabilities and disabling health issues; families on public assistance; families receiving support from relatives; and families from cities who have occupied abandoned and substandard rural housing. Many in some communities are recent immigrants.

An outsider looking at things from the vantage point of a large city would probably argue that rural communities are basically homogeneous after all, at least in terms of lacking much in the way of racial and ethnic diversity. To people in rural communities, though, it is the diversity they experience firsthand that matters, especially the visible differences that set people apart in terms of the work they do, the standard of living they enjoy, and whether they live in a lavish home on the edge of town or a subsistence rental in a rundown section of town.

It being untrue, then, that "everyone here is the same," people in small communities are nevertheless able to maintain the fiction that they are for several reasons. One is that the gentry typically live below their means—or find ways to downplay their wealth. A wealthy farmer we talked with, for example, drives a beat-up pickup and does his own fieldwork. A doctor who lives in an upscale house tries to avoid further conspicuous consumption by driving an ordinary car and going out of town to purchase anything fancy. A second reason is that many of the gentry we talked with make a point of interacting on an equal basis with other townspeople, who in turn appreciate this fact. A wageworker we spoke with, for instance, said he respected one of the wealthiest men in town because the man would sit beside him at the café and chat like anyone else.

A third reason people feel equal is the lack of clear distinctions between blue-collar and white-collar occupations. Farmers and construction workers, for example, who do manual labor often earn as much as office workers. Some of them have been to college while some of the white-collar business owners and administrators have not been. The occupations in which women work blend across class lines as well. A woman we talked with who works in a retail store, for example, says she must dress upscale but probably earns less than some of the long-term office workers. Finally, the limited opportunities for social interaction in small places force people to mingle on an equal footing. They go to the same church, send their children to the same school, and buy groceries at the same store.

As people in rural communities see it, these opportunities for mingling are one of the perks that sets them apart from people in cities and suburbs. When you live in a large place, they say, you can isolate yourself from people unlike yourself if you want to, but in rural communities you can't, which, they think, means coming to accept people as equals despite their differences. As Mr. Somers puts it, "In a small town, it's so damn small that you encounter all groups, okay?"

These reasons for feeling that everyone is in it together if not actually the same contribute to the sense that the community is home. Like a family, the members are different, yet they have a common bond. The commonalities of living in the same place and in some respects sharing a common destiny allow them to think of the community as an entity they share.

There is a darker side to the togetherness townspeople experience, though. Just as among kin groups, there is a strong sense of "us" and "them." It seems to "us" that we know each other and are all the same because "us" excludes "them." The excluded don't belong. They are the newcomers of different ancestry who don't quite fit in, the poor who townspeople figure are on welfare and probably up to no good, the teenagers whose names appear on the police report.

Exclusion of this kind is nothing new in small towns. New England towns like Newborough deported transients in the eighteenth century who could not pull their weight financially, committed petty crimes, or got pregnant out of wedlock. Southern towns like Gulfdale kept African Americans in segregated housing. Fairfield was one of the many frontier communities settled as ethnically homogeneous colonies.

The townspeople we spoke with liked to describe their community as a big, happy family. But their comments betrayed the limits of that inclusiveness. "Did you participate in 4-H or Future Farmers of America?" we asked one of the Midwesterners we interviewed. "No," he replied, "they wouldn't let Mexicans do that!" "I've been called a beaner, a wetback, a spic," he added. "At least they didn't burn our house down."

A farmer of German American heritage told us he'd be glad to hire some Hispanic workers if he could just trust them, but didn't feel he could. They'd probably wreck something or get in trouble. He'd purchased a huge tractor so he could do all the work himself. "They just come here looking for free stuff," he said. "We need to stop them at the border."

A truck farmer in a town that was nearly 50 percent Hispanic was proud of the diversity in his community and acknowledged that the apples and cherries on his farm depended on Hispanic labor. But he too thought more should be done to keep Hispanics out. They need to be stopped at the border, he said.

Social scientists call this kind of exclusion "othering." It ranges from negative stereotypes to overt discrimination. By no means do all rural Americans engage in it. But it was one of the ways the subjects I interviewed maintained their sense of identity. They probably revealed more than they realized when they said the people they knew were all the same.

COMMUNITY SPIRIT

The lighter side of community spirit in rural places is a function of rituals, symbols, and stories as well as the implicit norms and understandings people share. Every town I studied had a community ritual. Gulfdale's Christmas parade, as Mr. Cahill mentioned, was its annual ritual. The weather in Gulfdale in December was usually warm enough that people in the town and surrounding villages came in droves to watch or participate. Other towns held rituals, sometimes lasting for several days or an entire week, that marked the seasons or reminded people of the town's ethnic heritage. It was a tomato festival in one community, the dogwood festival in another, an Oktoberfest in another, and an Old Home Week in yet another. Some of the events coincided with the homecoming football game or the county fair. Typical activities ranged from pie-eating contests and tractor pulls to barn dances and outdoor concerts.

The sociologist Randall Collins suggests that rituals like these contribute to community spirit in multiple ways. They bring people out of their homes, giving them an opportunity to interact with community members they might not ordinarily see and to do so in a festive, non-businesslike atmosphere. People's physical co-presence, Collins claims, encourages an implicit awareness of the social norms they have in common. In addition, co-presence is conducive to shared feelings that may be harder to express in other contexts. There is a sense of spontaneity that nevertheless reflects what people have learned to do and say on previous occasions.[8]

Rural festivals heighten residents' sense of living in a uniquely special place, just as professional football teams, renowned orchestras, and famous landmarks do for cities. Townspeople usually see the humor in their community being known for the largest ball of twine or the most colorful ceramic jackrabbits, but even the jokes give them something to talk about.

The stories people in rural places tell about their communities come in two varieties. There are the official stories that make up the town or county's history. In past years when small communities had newspapers, these histories were often published to coincide with major anniversaries of the community's founding. Many of these are now preserved on local websites. Most of the towns I visited of any size had historical centers or libraries with local memorabilia and a few had self-designated local historians who heeded the call from time to time for public lectures. Maybe it was the lack of much else to do, but townspeople even turned out in reasonable numbers to visit the local historical center and listen to their town's history being recounted yet again. Newborough's local historians (a couple in their early seventies), for instance, had a well-practiced narrative they had given many times and were happy to give again.

The other genre of local lore includes what city people would call urban legends. Many of these stories, such as the one about the largest fish ever caught in the lake or the time people spotted a flying saucer, were apocryphal. Many of the others were not. The most common of these are narratives about good deeds. For instance, one of the people we spoke with in Newborough recalled the "hell of a snowstorm" they'd had several years ago. "I've got a pretty good snow blower that can handle just about anything, but this storm was too much for it. Well, the chap across the street has a very large garden tractor with a huge snow blower on the front of it. He blew the whole damn street. Everybody's sidewalk. Everybody's driveway. Now, that's a neighborly thing!"

I suppose it stretches the meaning of ritual to include community planning meetings under that rubric; and yet, townspeople frequently described them that way. For example, Newborough's civic leaders realized a few years ago that tourism could be a source of community vitality. There were some caves in the hills and the hills could draw tourists in the fall. The difficulty was that some central planning needed to happen. A group formed, and what it discovered was that the meetings themselves brought people together and generated community spirit.

Besides the stories and rituals, symbols are a big part of community spirit in rural places. To an outsider, most buildings in rural communities offer little to boast about. They nevertheless symbolize the community's identity. The grain elevator with the town's name emblazoned near the top serves this purpose in Fairfield. The water tower does in Newborough. The historic courthouse does in Gulfdale. In other communities, identities are commemorated in the depot-turned-museum, the renovated residence of the town's first mayor, and the community project that has "beautified" the oldest buildings on Main Street.

The most revered building in town is usually the school. The building may have seen better days, or, in other cases, it represents the result of a significant recent financial investment. In either case the school is the same one many of the townspeople attended as children and where parents went for teacher conferences, PTA meetings, annual band and choir concerts, and athletic events.

Athletic events are stereotypically the hallmarks of small towns. People turn out for football and basketball games in large numbers. The team in effect represents the community. A winning season swells community pride. A losing season leaves it depressed. Rural communities are hardly as insular as the stereotype suggests, though. People enjoy getting away, too. The ones who can afford it take trips to Paris, New York, and San Francisco, where they attend concerts and plays and visit museums. "If you like high school athletics," one resident lamented, "this is a great place to be, but in terms of concerts, artists coming here, lecture series, we just don't have that."

MIDDLE CLASS

The examples I've described in this chapter demonstrate the considerable extent to which people in rural areas view their communities like they do their own homes. The community is home because they know people (or feel they do) and interact with them on a regular enough basis that they feel they can be trusted. To be sure, the people they know are older or younger than they are, in better or worse health, have children in school or their children are grown and gone, and they work in different occupations or are homemakers or retired. There is nevertheless an affinity because of the place in which they live and what it stands for in their minds. Their various interests notwithstanding, they know the norms of the community well enough to abide by them without having to give them much thought. A common identity is publicly affirmed in the stories they tell and the events in which they participate. These relationships, obligations, and common understandings are what I have called the "moral community."

No community ever quite lives up to its potential of being a home, any more than a family's home does. In referring to them as moral communities I do not mean to idealize them. The communities I studied included people who rarely interacted with their neighbors and preferred not to. The community was a stopping place before they moved on. Clearly people who said they knew everyone in town didn't and the ones who said everyone was the same were failing to see the differences.

Before adopting a cynical view of rural communities, though, it is worth a moment's reflection to consider that the way of life they express isn't far from what has always been considered the hallmarks of the American middle class. Apart from small communities being small, the norms they espouse pertain to a large share of the population that includes blue-collar and white-collar occupations. The norms encourage treating people (at least people like you) equally and getting to know them, and rewarding hard work and personal responsibility. Being part of a community means caring about it enough to want it to be preserved. In these respects, rural communities are part of the culture of middle-class America that many observers say is currently threatened by policies that blatantly favor the rich at the expense of everyone else.

To summarize, moral communities consist of a geographic space, a population that considers itself to be a part of this community, extensive social interaction within this population, an institutional structure comprised of formal and informal leadership, a sense of boundedness that separates insiders from outsiders, stories and rituals that affirm the nature of this boundedness, and everyday practices that verbally and behaviorally reinforce common norms about persons' obligations to themselves, their neighbors, and the community.[9] A moral community in these respects is enabling in terms of the expectations its members reliably take for granted and at the same time is constraining in terms of the beliefs and activities it encourages and the ones it discourages. The key point about rural communities, understood in this way, is that the people who live in them are not individuals who make up their minds about issues and elections based on only individually held economic interests or personal anxieties. The communities in which they live influence them as well, defining the moral fabric of what they consider to be right and good. It matters greatly, therefore, if people perceive—correctly or incorrectly—that the communities upholding their way of life are in danger.

2

Present Dangers

The stories rural people tell about their communities demonstrate how much the problems they face differ from place to place. Some of the problems of course affect large swaths of the rural population. Government statistics capture a slice of them, but when you add what people say they experience, you see things in a different light. People have dealt with many of the problems before, and they've made accommodations that were never quite as satisfactory as they had hoped—waiting another year to paint the house, dining at McDonalds, driving farther to see the doctor. These contribute to the frustrations simmering in rural America. In addition, the cumulative impact of rural communities' problems—even the ones people say aren't that serious—frequently betray a fear that the way of life they know and value is in danger. Each of these—what the statistics show and don't show, the specific problems, and the fears about their way of life—require understanding if we are to grasp what is taking place in these communities.

Statistical reports of rural-urban differences drew interest following the 2016 presidential election. Many of the figures show the disadvantages of being a rural person living in a sparsely populated town or county. If you live in one of these places your community is probably shrinking while the urban population is growing, which suggests that people are leaving your community to live in cities and suburbs; and while cities and suburbs are attracting immigrants, your community isn't. Besides that, rural people like you are older, less educated, and even if they weren't older would still be less educated. Furthermore, your communities have significantly higher teenage pregnancy rates than urban places. Your health and health facilities aren't as good. And even though you occupy a huge portion of the nation's land and therefore have a disproportionate influence in politics, you contribute far less to the national economy than urban people do.

To anyone who took a high school or college social studies class these differences will seem familiar. In 1810, 95 percent of the U.S. population was rural; in 1910, 55 percent was; and in 2010, that number declined to only 20 percent. Students contemplating these figures have no difficulty grasping the implications. Urbanization is the significant social trend now and in the past. Cities and suburbs are where the action is. Rural communities are falling behind.

Interesting as these rural-urban comparisons are, how they matter depends less on national generalizations than on local manifestations. That rural population is declining relative to urban population, for instance, misses the fact that population in absolute terms is growing in many rural communities, holding steady in others, and declining seriously in others. The experiences of people living in these communities are thus quite different. Perceptions, you realize in talking with people, matter as much as or more than raw statistics.

Even the statistics mask some important considerations that demographers know should be considered. For one thing, the

U.S. Census Bureau has changed its definition of "rural" and "urban" enough that long-term comparisons are sometimes misleading. For another, rural counties that grow enough or are close enough to expanding cities become reclassified as urban, leaving the ones that remain rural less likely to have grown. And for another, population decline in absolute terms is a function of factors that vary from place to place, including rates of natural increase, in-migration, and out-migration.

These considerations notwithstanding, stagnant and declining population is the reality that many rural towns and counties have been facing over the past quarter century, if not longer. Whether they say they are happy living in a small place that is not growing, which many do, or wish their community was larger, a declining population is worrisome to many of the people you meet in rural America. They know it can signal a loss of jobs and tax revenue, the departure of friends and family members, and greater difficulties keeping local businesses from closing.

POPULATION DECLINE

The most serious causes of population decline in rural communities are man-made and natural disasters. Picher, Oklahoma's population of 1,600 people, for instance, was evacuated in 2010 because of contamination from 70 million tons of mine tailings and 36 million tons of toxic sludge. Church's Ferry, North Dakota, lost 90 percent of its population because a series of wet seasons increased the size of nearby Devil's Lake. McMullen, Alabama's population fled from Hurricane Katrina and only ten people returned.

Other towns of course have experienced natural disasters and survived. Greensburg, Kansas, for instance, determined to rebuild after it was decimated in 2007 by a deadly tornado, and a decade later its population had recovered to about half its original size. Ken Somers's town of Newborough was completely flooded several years ago, yet its population is only marginally smaller than it was. Mr. Cahill's town of Gulfdale has replenished the population it was losing because Hurricane Katrina drove people from the coast inland.

Apart from natural disasters and other traumatic events, rural communities are confronted with systemic challenges that cause many to lose population. The smallest towns are hardest hit. Nationally, there were approximately 9,000 incorporated towns or boroughs with populations of fewer than a thousand residents in 1980; by 2010 the population of 62 percent of these communities was smaller. That was true of 48 percent of the 2,800 communities with a thousand but fewer than two thousand residents in 1980. And it was true of 42 percent of the 2,600 communities with two thousand but fewer than five thousand residents in 1980.[1]

Larger rural communities generally did better in terms of holding population or growing. Nevertheless, 41 percent of the 1,100 rural communities with populations of five thousand to ten thousand in 1980 were smaller in 2010, as were 38 percent of the 6,600 communities with ten thousand to twenty-five thousand. In all, nearly 15 million people were living in rural communities with declining populations, and these towns were serving at least another 15 million people living in their immediate vicinity.

But population statistics do not begin to capture what it means to people living there when their communities experience significant decline. Between 2008 and 2010, I made several research trips to Lebanon, Kansas, to see what I could learn firsthand and from talking with people there. Lebanon was the geographic center of the United States, or so it was generally considered to be when engineers for the U.S. Coast and Geodetic Survey in 1898 pasted a U.S. map on a piece of cardboard and found that Lebanon was where it balanced. Writers have visited it ever since to learn what they can about rural America. At the turn of the millennium, for instance, a writer for the *Washington Post* spent a day in Lebanon, absorbed by its silence and overwhelmed by its emptiness. Main Street stays so vacant, he wrote, that "a dog could lie down in it for a long nap in no fear of being awakened, much less run over."[2] That was true when I visited a few years later. I have a photo on my office wall of a crumbling three-story building on Main Street that once served as a bank. It speaks volumes of what has happened to the town. In 1880, more than sixteen hundred people lived here; today fewer than two hundred do.[3]

Even though its residents call it home, an unspoken sadness pervades Lebanon. The newest houses were built in the 1950s. The Methodist church and the grain elevator are about the only places still in business. Shuttered buildings give the business district an aura of neglect—what sociologist Robert J. Sampson has called the "broken windows" effect in rundown urban neighborhoods.[4] Long-time residents, most of them with gray hair, gather at the café on quiet mornings to discuss the weather and grain prices.

They warm to a stranger from the East Coast interested in their town. The stories are of long ago, about the preacher in the community's early days who painted Bible verses in large letters on the grain elevator and the religious sect from Chicago that recruited some of the locals to start a colony near Jerusalem. They remember when the town had a bowling alley and a movie theater and can point to the vacant lot where the hardware store was once located. These are the legends in their telling at the café that commemorate the community's identity.

Were a visitor only to stop at towns the size of Lebanon, the picture of rural America would indeed be bleak. In the scores of towns I visited that had populations under a thousand the story was much the same. Ramshackle houses with plastic taped over broken windows, rusted vehicles in gravel driveways, an occasional farm machine in a backyard, and weeds in vacant lots. But towns even a bit larger, as the census figures suggest, were mixed. About half were declining and about half were holding their own.

Smith Center is several miles due west of Lebanon. I spent time there as well. Its population has declined from twenty-two hundred in 1980 to about sixteen hundred. But it is the county seat and is the only town of its size in a 30-mile radius. Compared with Lebanon the town is a bustle of activity. Farmers come to do business at the bank and the John Deere dealership and to file reports at the county agricultural office. An online insurance business is thriving. Tourists drive over to see the spot a few miles from town where "Home on the Range" was composed. And there is a large high school on the edge of town. A few years ago, Smith Center made headlines in the *New York Times* because its football team set a national record, winning four consecutive state championships and scoring 78 points in one game during the first quarter.

Even though Smith Center's population decline worries its residents, they express a great deal of pride in their community—and not only because of the football team. The high school has a stellar graduation rate and most of its students go on to college. A new subdivision has attracted retirees. A younger couple from a city started a bed and breakfast a few years ago. A local entrepreneur is said to have earned multiple millions of dollars starting a technology company.

Smith Center is not unique in having benefited from government offices and local entrepreneurs. Ethanol plants, mining ventures, sustainable energy wind generation projects, organic farms, prisons, and high-tech companies have contributed to the survival of many rural communities.

The larger pattern in small towns, though, is either of population stagnation or decline, often coupled with economic hardship. Besides the fact that many rural communities were already small, and had already been declining, they have been affected in recent decades by several nationwide trends, one of the most significant of which is the changing nature of agriculture.

In the nineteenth century, when many of these towns were founded, their sole reason to exist was to service the needs of the farmers who lived an easy horse-and-wagon distance away and to provide coal and water for the steam-driven trains that connected the farms to the outside world. During the twentieth century the smallest communities diminished as a result of improved roads, trucks and automobiles, and diesel-powered trains—what one writer has called "death by dieselization."[5]

A century ago approximately six million Americans farmed. Today, fewer than 750,000 employed Americans list their principal occupation as farmer. The reasons for this decline are well known. The Great Depression had an impact, although not as great as sometimes imagined, because farm families usually had no better option than to hunker in place. When servicemen returned from World War II, the farm population temporarily swelled, but the 1950s saw the departure of thousands of marginal farmers whose means were insufficient to support the purchase of tractors and machinery. The Carter administration's grain embargo against the Soviet Union and inflated fuel prices in the late 1970s and early 1980s were a major setback. In recent decades, larger and more powerful equipment has enabled fewer farmers to farm significantly more acres. As the number of farmers fell, the size of farm families also declined, leaving fewer people to live in or near small towns or to need people in those communities to operate farm-related businesses.[6]

John and Karen Meeks, who farm near Fairfield, are an example of these changes. They farm approximately ten times as much land as Karen's parents did in the 1950s. Although most of it is rented, they consider themselves fortunate to have had aunts and uncles and neighbors to rent from whose children did not want to farm. In the 1980s it took John and his father-in-law more than a week with the help of several seasonal field hands to complete the wheat harvest each summer. The combine he now uses cuts as much wheat in an hour as his old combine cut in a day. He harvests more than twice as many acres in half the time.

The Meeks anticipate even fewer farmers will be needed in the future. They don't expect the next generation of Meeks to farm. Some of their neighbors have already purchased GPS-guided tractors and combines. The farmer can sit in the air-conditioned tractor cab doing computer work and making cell phone calls while the tractor basically drives itself. The combine's onboard computer monitors the moisture content and yield of each quarter acre and prepares a report for next year's planting and fertilizer.

Besides these changes in agriculture, rural communities' population dynamics are conditioned by other factors. Populations fare better in towns that had the good fortune of being located near interstate highways and in communities that happen to be the location of a small liberal arts or community college. Fairfield has benefited in both these respects. Fairfield, Newborough, and Gulfdale have all benefited from being county seats. County seats hold population better because people go there to conduct business. Smaller towns usually fare worse if there is a larger town in the same county. They do better, though, if they are close enough to a city for people to commute.

Newborough is an interesting case in point. Despite it being the county seat, people we talked to in Newborough felt the community was dying, as evidenced by its recent population decline, and would continue to die because residents were increasingly traveling to other communities to work and to shop and to see the doctor or consult with a financial advisor. The services that an aging population increasingly needed were unavailable in Newborough, and in good weather at least it was easy for everyone to hop in the car and go 20 miles to another town for this and that. "There's no way in hell Newborough is going to keep a substantial business district," a long-time resident lamented.

Evidence also demonstrates that rural communities do better demographically if there are other reasons for people to live there besides farming. Nearly 80 percent of rural communities in which the primary economic activity is farming have

lost population since 1980, whereas fewer than 30 percent
have where the economic base is human and social services.
It matters, too, if rural communities offer lifestyle amenities,
such as lakes, rivers, foothills, and warmer climates that attract tourists and retirees. More than 70 percent of communities ranking lowest on a 7-point amenity scale have lost
population, compared to 15 percent of communities ranking
highest.[7]

Although they knew it was happening, many of the people
we spoke with were surprisingly complacent about their communities losing population. The decline had been occurring
long enough and slowly enough in many communities that
people said they hardly noticed. Some of them were like the
Fairfield residents Ms. Meeks described who didn't want new
people to move in. Families with children nearly always said
they'd prefer their children go to college and get a better job
even if that meant moving away. Younger people who had
stayed and those who had moved away generally said their
parents may have wanted them to stay but left the decision
to them.

But saying they were complacent, I learned, missed important nuances in what people were trying to communicate. They
were older, lifelong residents who missed the drugstore they
used to walk to, but they still felt the community was a good
place to live. They were like the folks in Smith Center who
knew the declining population was making it harder to field a
star football team, but they refused to say the community was
losing vitality. There was as much community spirit as ever.

The ones who agreed their town was declining didn't always have population in mind, either. It was more that they
hankered for the "good ol' days" when there was a "five and

dime" store, a carousel in the park, and the community had its own brass band. They said Main Street didn't look as good as it used to and the streets were in ill repair. They wished the police would patrol more regularly and hoped the neighbors would soon get around to removing the dead tree. Had they thought about it, they probably would have said that a lot of urban neighborhoods were declining in those ways too.

There was more anger and frustration in rural communities, though, than complacency. People knew that tornadoes and hailstorms and floods could wreak havoc on the local economy, but it made them mad that businesses closed and families left because it took so long to get help. Newborough was one of the communities that rebounded quickly. The town manager in another New England state said her community was less fortunate. The state provided no assistance at all. FEMA's response was slow in coming. The local police did what they could to keep track of victims and protect their property until they could return.

The unanticipated result of the flood was that the community's politics shifted dramatically, she said. Before the flood, the town's elected officials were making progress toward halting its demographic decline by attracting tourists and securing a block grant for affordable housing and a couple of small businesses. The flood put those efforts on hold and necessitated an increase in local taxes. "People here are pretty angry," she responded when asked about the political climate. There had always been a mixture of Democrats and Republicans. But now there were conservative Republicans who were not only angry but "very vocal" about expressing it.

Besides having to deal with natural disasters, Walmart was perhaps the most frequent focus of anger, even though many people admitted shopping there. Mr. Cahill, for instance, said the business at his grocery store in Gulfdale had declined significantly since Walmart came. One of his neighbors who grew watermelons besides working for the utility company was mad at Walmart for undercutting his income. Mr. Somers in Newborough had managed only somewhat better in keeping a niche separate from Walmart. The Meeks in Fairfield were among the few who were unambiguously happy to have a Walmart in town.

Franchise chains, the Internet, and online shopping giant Amazon evoked anger too. The mom-and-pop hardware store had closed because of a Home Depot in a larger town 30 miles away. John Deere shut down the local dealership to run a more economical operation in a larger town. It was cheaper to order household goods and farm supplies online than to purchase them locally.

The Internet, Walmart, and even having cable news and talk shows available 24/7 were all convenient—and people who would have been isolated in their rural communities a generation or two ago were glad to have these links to the outside world. Having the outside world right in their midst, however, also contributed to their sense that the world was changing and leaving them behind. Decline meant putting up with slow DSL Internet connections instead of high-speed service. It was having phone lines that rarely worked when weather was bad.

The outside world being so readily accessible was a source of worry, too. You could feel your children were at risk from what they could access on the Internet. The mother of two boys in their teens who lived in a town of thirty-five hundred, for example, told us she and the other parents she knew there had a "sense of fear." We get "glimpses of changes that are going on in the culture at large," she said, "and then those things start popping up in our little community." A few years later a triple homicide occurred in her town over a dispute about drugs.

Complicit as they were in many of these changes, residents didn't always call what they were feeling anger. They said there was a sense of loss, a feeling of grief. They felt beleaguered but also considered themselves survivors. Better to be angry than depressed, they said. It took grit to stand against the world—"a fighting mentality," a rugged West Texan said.

However, sometimes the anger festered to the point that even the people we talked to found it hard to understand. People in one community had been angry for years because the highway department refused to put a sign on the interstate directing travelers into town. Another community felt "sold out" when the town's police department merged with the county sheriff's office.

BRAIN DRAIN

Besides population loss, a second problem evident in national statistics is lower education levels in rural than in urban areas. These differences are troubling at both the state and local levels. The "brain drain," as Patrick J. Carr and Maria J. Kefalas demonstrated clearly in *Hollowing Out the Middle*, is depleting rural states of talent and tax dollars. Rural states and towns are left without college-trained young people to provide healthcare, teach, run high-tech businesses, and implement the latest agricultural innovations.[8]

States' capacity to meet the challenge is often limited. Tight budgets force in-state tuition increases and reductions in funding for colleges and universities. States' ability to retain college graduates also depends on local employment opportunities. South Dakota and Iowa, for instance, consistently lose college graduates to Minneapolis-St. Paul. Missouri and Kansas compete to attract businesses to their side of Kansas City.[9] Even states that do reasonably well at providing in-state job opportunities, though, experience net loss from rural communities to urban communities. College-educated people also leave the state because they have attended college elsewhere and discovered more appealing parts of the country in which to live.

Retaining young people who earn college degrees is pretty much a lost cause in most rural communities, people told us. "It's definitely a brain drain here," a preacher we talked with in Newborough explained, for example. "Among the ones who have a high school degree, many of them stay," he said. "A two-year degree at a local community college down the road, some stay and some leave. But any of the kids who have anything going with a four-year degree, they're gone." That robs the community of talent, he says, and contributes to its economic decline.

A student of mine from North Dakota put a fine point on it when I asked if she planned to return to Fargo when she graduated. "That's a scary thought!" she exclaimed.

Were a visitor to start in Fargo and drive west or north for an hour, the route would pass through some of the state's most productive farmland and some of its smallest towns. Homesteaders settled here in the 1880s about the time the Northern Pacific Railroad was built. By 1910, four of the towns had populations of more than a thousand, and those towns held their own until the 1970s, but have declined since then. The smaller towns were already declining. Today, long stretches of soybean fields are punctuated with scattered shelterbelts, an occasional rural cemetery, and a few well-kept farmsteads. The typical town has several shops along Main Street, a few churches and filling stations, and a water tower. The larger towns have a high school that sends a share of its graduates on to college. But these are not the places for college graduates to find jobs.

John and Cheryl Linden live in one of these communities. The town called itself Lincoln City in the 1880s but picked the more modest name of Sharon a decade later. The town is large enough to have a church and a farmers' co-op, but townspeople drive to a larger town to buy groceries and go to the doctor. Mr. and Mrs. Linden both have four-year college degrees. He farms the 240 acres that have been in the family for four generations—small by local standards, he says—and she is employed full-time as a technologist at a hospital 20 miles away. It is not unusual for farmers in their community to have college degrees, they say. A generation ago, farm incomes were sufficient for farmers to send their children to college, often as a hedge against the harder times they expected would come. With two incomes, the Lindens have sent all five of their children to college. But none of them farm and only one of them lives in North Dakota.

North Dakota has done what it can to keep its college-educated young people, especially by offering high-quality low-cost in-state college tuition and by promoting economic development in Fargo and Grand Forks. Oil production in the Bakken Formation in the western part of the state has also generated a few white-collar jobs. For people like the

Lindens, though, the brain drain is personal—and is a difficult pill to swallow. They anticipated their children leaving to
find jobs in distant cities. They did not anticipate how their
children's friends would view them when they went to visit.
"You're looked down on," Mr. Linden says. "You know, L'il
Abner. Clem Kadiddlehopper."

Mrs. Linden says it makes her angry to hear these remarks.
"It was always the dumb one who stayed home and farmed."
The "brain drain" meant that everyone else who could go
away did. "The dumb ones weren't going to make it," so they
stayed. And that's not true anymore, she says. You've got to
be smart, educated, forward-looking to make it in farming,
but that's not the stereotype.

Falling behind in educational attainment smacks especially
deep in communities like the Lindens'. Rural communities
from Ohio to Minnesota and Iowa were known as the "education belt" well into the twentieth century. Townspeople still
take pride in high rates of high school graduation. They feel
demeaned when outsiders look down on them, calling them
"hicks" and "country bumpkins." It bothers them to read
books and articles casting them as gullible, slow-minded, and
eccentric. And sometimes they admit to feeling inferior themselves, like the farmer who said he just feels "dumb" working
as hard as he does and earning so little.

How their children are doing in school is another source
of pride—or embarrassment. Small towns are fishbowls. The
teachers and principals we talked to knew they were being
judged by how well the students performed on standard-
ized tests and spelling bees as well as in sports. Parents know
whose children are going on to college and whose aren't. The
ones who don't tell stories of missed opportunities.

As community symbols, the schools staying open or closing is one of the most telling markers of how people think the community is doing. Residents in one of the mining towns we studied remembered when children's laughter from the schoolyard could be heard throughout the town. Now the silence told them the town was dying. In another community, a resident spoke emotionally of losing the school. "It was just like they took the heart out of our town. People no longer had a regular place to go."

The brain drain story is more complicated than rural people lamenting the loss of schools and saying goodbye to their college-educated offspring, though. In interview after interview I learned about the "frog pond" effect that young people experience in rural communities. Growing up in a small community makes it possible, as the saying goes, to be "a big frog in a small pond," which can result in an unrealistic appraisal of one's talents and perhaps a rude awakening when thrown at some point into a larger pond. The first chair trumpet player in the high school band, for instance, finds it hard to make the cut for a large university band, and the star football player now working for a large corporation is no longer a celebrity.

The frog pond is an example of how moral communities generate strong implicit loyalties to the point that they constrain people in ways that may have detrimental effects on their career aspirations. Durkheim wrote of these constraints as sources of what he called "altruistic suicide"—suicides committed because of over-absorption into a community.[10] The frog pond is nothing of this sort, yet for people in small communities it speaks to the fact that the community easily becomes a dominant point of reference. A high school student, for example, may make excellent grades in a small school but be unprepared for the competition in a university. Similarly, a student in a community with no scientists, actors, and engineers may fail to imagine any of those careers being possible.

The frog pond effect was of special concern to the teachers, principals, and superintendents we interviewed. They found it frustrating that bright students sold themselves short, following the influence of peers, and planning to pursue vocational careers instead of four-year college degrees. From talking with people who had gone to college and left small towns for jobs in cities, we also learned of the difficulties that many rural first-generation college students experience. They experienced culture shock from being among a sizable number of people in a large community for the first time, feeling isolated and unsure of how to make friends. Choosing majors was frequently a challenge, too, because there was no one in their hometown or family with any idea of what was marketable and how to match interests with career expectations.

The educational disadvantages of rural communities also cannot be addressed fully without considering textbook controversies over the teaching of evolution. In the 1990s, school boards in several rural states came under withering criticism from scientists and national education associations for laws requiring that the biblical story of creation be taught alongside or instead of evolution. The criticism suggested that students in these states would not be properly prepared for college and for jobs in the professions. The criticism also suggested that intelligent people who wanted the best educations for their children would shun living in these states. The issue had more to do with states than with local communities. However, there was some evidence that local communities mattered because school board elections often had low turn-out, which made it possible for candidates from small towns to win with relatively little investment. In Kansas, where the debate about teaching evolution went back and forth for more than a decade, two of the most outspoken creationists on the board were from small towns.

In Oklahoma, where the first legislation against teaching evolution occurred in 1923, the ban continued with the support of fundamentalist preachers into the 1960s, when the U.S. Supreme Court ruled against teaching creationism. Under the rubric of "intelligent design," opponents of evolution reopened the issue in the mid-1990s and throughout the next two decades introduced bill after bill requiring evolution to be taught as a theory and creation to be taught as an alternate theory in the name of academic freedom.[11]

It seemed only reasonable, those involved in these debates said, to teach both sides, especially when the evidence for evolution was, in their view, so flimsy. As one of the small-town pastors we talked with explained, "Evolution has never been proved to be more than a theory and there ought to be equal time for the theory of creation." He added, "Those who would push evolution have gone about their skimpy research and drawing conclusions from very little data, grasping at straws to prove their point."

For parents who had thought much about the issue, they mostly agreed that teaching both creation and evolution was the commonsense, open-minded approach and thus favored it. Teachers and principals fell on both sides of the issue, some deeply concerned about the backward anti-science image their community and state was presenting to the world, and yet the ones who favored clearer teaching about evolution as science often said it was risky to run up against conservative local opinion by speaking out.

TEEN PREGNANCY

Teen pregnancy rates that exceed those in urban areas are another issue of concern in many rural communities. A national report produced by the Centers for Disease Control and Prevention showed that there were 18.9 births for every 1,000 women between the ages of fifteen and nineteen in counties with large urban populations, while in rural counties there were 30.9 births per 1,000 women in the same age group. The report did not examine the effect that attitudes about abortion may have had, but did provide several additional comparisons. The teen birthrate fell between 2007 and 2015 in rural communities just as it did in larger communities. And, as was true in larger communities, the teen birthrate in rural communities varied by race and ethnicity. Among non-Latina white teens, the 2015 birthrate in rural counties was 26.8 per thousand, among non-Latina black teens it was 39.6 per thousand, and among Latina women it was 47 per thousand.[12]

Teen births have long been considered a problem because of the frequent difficulties teen parents have in providing effective financial support. The higher-than-average teen birthrates in rural communities are a matter of concern locally as well as in national headlines, despite several mitigating factors that the statistics hide, the most notable of which is that relatively smaller proportions of rural communities are teens than is true in larger communities. Nevertheless, my research showed that parents and teachers in rural communities viewed promiscuous sex, teen pregnancy, and early marriage as deeply disturbing problems. Even if the incidence of these problems was rare, vigilance to protect against them was ever-present.

One reason was that abortion was generally not an acceptable option. When a teenager became pregnant, she was expected to keep the baby, often with the assistance of her parents, or put the baby up for adoption. In either case, she was stigmatized for having had sex out of wedlock and for not being more responsible. The local grapevine spread gossip quickly.

A second concern was that early marriage (between ages sixteen and twenty-one) significantly reduced the likelihood of going to college for both men and women. In 1960 before birth control, for example, rural men who married early were only 26 percent as likely to go to college as men who did not marry early, and women were only 13 percent as likely as women who did not marry early. And thirty years later the odds were only slightly improved. Men who married early were about 32 percent as likely to go to college as men who did not marry early, and women were only 24 percent as likely.[13]

One of the women we talked with remembered clearly what had happened in her case. She dreamed of being the first person in her family to go to college, hoping to become a teacher, but she and her girlfriends "got interested in boys and that kind of went out the window." She and her future husband dated in high school and got married a month after graduation.

The culture of small towns is the other reason teen pregnancy and early marriage worry people in these communities. They know the neighbors will gossip. They know from family stories in many cases how early marriage affected them and their neighbors. They understand that the climate in high schools where the chances of going on to college may be small encourages early dating. The compact that maintains the moral culture of the community is also broken. People are supposed to take responsibility for themselves. They are to uphold time-worn standards of moral decency.

It would be wrong, though, to conclude that rural people are moral prigs just waiting to shun the next young couple they hear about getting pregnant and having to get married. Instead, they blamed the promiscuous culture that was invading their communities through television and the Internet and they blamed themselves for not doing a better job of protecting their communities. That was their biggest source of frustration.

When Brenda Wiggins talked with us, she was in her mid-fifties. Her children were grown and had put themselves through college. They no longer lived in the community of fifteen thousand where she had lived all her life. She had married right out of high school and was pleased that her children had waited. She wasn't about to condemn the young people she knew who were getting married early. But she was disgusted at the temptations being put in their way.

"I get so angry," she said. "I live in the middle of a rural community that's basically pretty wholesome, right? But down the road not more than twenty minutes there's an adult bookstore with all this X-rated nudie stuff. There's porno all over the place. No wonder families are falling apart. But what are we doing about it? Nothing!"

The remedies people thought should work didn't seem to be helping as much as people hoped, from what they said. Those were teaching good morals at school and in the churches. The difficulty in schools was teachers fearing they would be fired if they refused to teach sex education classes or tried to talk about the Ten Commandments. The difficulty in churches was that rural pastors were finding it hard to get young people in their communities interested. Most of the parishioners were middle-aged or elderly and the churches were too small to have special programs for youth.

DRUGS

Rural Americans frequently say they prefer living in a small town because there is less crime than in a city. They feel safer and hope their children will not be exposed to drugs and violence. But small towns have never been entirely free of juvenile delinquency, hooliganism, alcoholism, and the occasional theft and murder. In the early 1990s, methamphetamine use became a problem of epidemic proportions in rural areas partly because of the ease with which meth labs could be hidden in sparsely populated places. Heroin addiction has become a problem of grave concern in rural communities since then. By 2014, data compiled by the CDC showed the rate of overdose deaths per 100,000 population was actually higher in rural areas than in large metropolitan areas.[14]

Before the heroin problem became as severe and well-publicized as it did, the perception that drug abuse was a serious community problem was already as widespread in rural communities as in metropolitan areas. A 1997 nationally representative survey, for instance, found that 47 percent of respondents in small, nonmetropolitan towns thought drug abuse was a serious problem in their community compared with 48 percent in metropolitan areas.[15]

Among the reasons drugs are of special concern in small towns is that the victims and their families are known personally by their townspeople. And if they are not known personally they are part of the gossip network that talks about them behind their back. One of the tragedies we heard about in Newborough was a twenty-four-year-old woman who died from a drug overdose who had a three-week-old baby next to her. They were prescription drugs and the three women who had given her the drugs were arrested. This had obviously been big news in the community. It hit people more than it might have in a city, they said, because they were acquainted with the woman who died and the women who were arrested.

An episode like that made people in Newborough concerned about what else was happening that maybe they didn't know about. "I heard there is a lot of heroin around," one of the people we spoke with said. "I haven't seen it. I can't tell you anybody that has died from it, but that's what I've heard." Another resident was reminded that she knew the mother of a boy who was addicted and was sent away. "You hear stuff like that," she said.

Community leaders in rural towns understand that drugs and crime stem from many sources—the availability of prescription opioids, drug traffickers who can earn a handsome living, inadequate policing, and addiction itself. The ones we interviewed almost to a person also argued that the demoralizing culture of small towns is a contributing factor. Drugs and crime that resulted from drugs were an outlet for people in their communities who felt they were stuck and going nowhere. It was similar, they thought, to problems in inner-city neighborhoods where unemployment, under-employment, and poverty rates were high.

Elijah Robinson is a business leader in Taylor Springs, a Southern community of eleven thousand that is 90 percent African American. He and his wife have lived here all their lives except when they were in college and he was in the military. They vividly remember going to segregated schools and being discriminated against when the town was run by its white minority. Things are better now, they say, but have a long way to go. Mrs. Robinson is a social worker and he taught school, served on the town council, and currently heads a job training program for youth. I was especially interested in his thoughts because the town had recently experienced four murders of young men and women in their teens and early twenties, all related to drugs. Mr. Robinson had been personally shaken by the events and was more than ready to talk about what he saw as their underlying sources.

"Every life is important and yet it seems that some in our community have become so desensitized that they allow something seemingly trivial to make them so angry that they commit murder and then they can't even put into words why they did it." Mr. Robinson was convinced that this inexplicable rage stemmed from something much deeper. "I think a lot of it has to do with the hopelessness and the lack of opportunities young people feel here in this community."

Drugs and crime are merely symptoms, he said. "When people feel that it doesn't matter what they do, when they know the quality of their life cannot change, it's at that point of hopelessness that people begin to hurt other people. People who feel hurt are more likely to hurt other people. It's that cycle of hurt. Until we can give people hope, nothing is going to change."

Giving people hope, though, is a tall order in towns that have limited opportunities for good jobs and for people who may feel stuck in place because they are caring for an aging relative or other family member.

Most of the communities we studied were trying to do what they could to combat drug use, but usually with limited results, even by the most optimistic accounts. In Newborough, for example, the school had initiated the D.A.R.E. (Drug Abuse Resistance Education) program, which residents considered to be an important step in the right direction because it squared with their conviction that good training was a shared responsibility of the community and families. The program nevertheless came in for criticism from some in the community who saw it as something from the outside that perhaps discouraged families from taking as much responsibility for their children as they should. As one critic explained, "It teaches kids about drugs. They know more about drugs than we do. I don't know if that's good." She thought maybe the only effective solution was for parents always to know their children's whereabouts and to know their children's friends.

LACK OF JOBS

Among the most common descriptions of rural communities from outsiders is the lack of jobs. This concern is clearly on the minds of people living in these communities. They mourn the loss of the town's only manufacturing plant, the families they know who have lost their jobs, and the young people who have left the community to find work. Whether the plant that closed was a mop factory on the edge of town or the hardware store on Main Street, the loss is an economic set-back for the community as well as for the families directly involved. It means a reduction of the community's tax base and is likely to have a ripple effect as families travel to other towns to work and to shop.

For Tommy Rohn, the problem in Gulfdale wasn't so much a lack of jobs but an absence of *good* jobs. He had come home from a long day working on electrical poles and was getting ready to feed the chickens when we caught up with him. Being poor ran in the family. "Hard times is coming," his daddy always said. They'd come when the house burned down when his daddy was a boy. They'd come in the thirties when his grandma worked in town to keep the farm from going under. And they'd come for Tommy when he had to work right out of high school and wait a decade to get married. He's thankful he's had the few acres that have stayed in the family and steady work, even though the pay is low. Most of his friends from high school and many of his neighbors were less fortunate. When the plant where they worked closed, they moved away.

Besides their economic impact, business closings and a lack of jobs are also of cultural significance in small towns. Because people know—or know *about*—many of their neighbors, the family that moves away is likely to be missed by some and talked about by others. The conversation can quickly shift from what happened to them to what *could* happen to me.

Mark Buchanan is an example. He is a successful white-collar employee who lives in Portsmouth, a Midwestern river town of ten thousand, and he has held the same job for thirty years. His wife is also employed and together they enjoy a comfortable middle-class lifestyle. They love the fact that they have only a five-minute commute to their jobs. Housing is in-expensive, they have friends, and run into people they know at the grocery store and the bank. The community has a long, proud history of being among the earliest in the state and in recent years has turned the riverfront into a tourist destina-tion. Yet when we interviewed him Mr. Buchanan was wor-ried and trying to be upbeat instead of angry. Median income in the community was 20 percent below the state average and unemployment was twice the state average. Two of the com-munity's largest employers—small agribusiness plants—had recently announced layoffs of 30 percent. Mr. Buchanan had five years to go before he could retire. He was afraid he might be next.

"You don't know what's going to happen," he said. "You go to work one day and they say, 'Hey we've got to let ten people go and you're one of them.' I know a bunch of people here who are close to retirement age and they are being let go. Their savings have dwindled dramatically. They thought they were going to be secure when it came time to retire and that's no longer the case."

He thought there was good reason to be afraid. "What's going to happen? It's easy to be disheartened. You have to work to keep your chin up and stay positive and not throw in the towel and get angry at the world."

Besides fear about themselves and others losing their jobs and what this might mean for the community, the loss of a business or a town's failure to attract a new business is a blow to the community's pride. It feels like the community itself has failed. The business was part of the community's identity, a physical landmark that may have been there for years and been operated by one of the town's prominent families. Now it was an empty hulk that reminded the community of better days.

Not that the community languishes in grief, but it makes matters worse knowing that the business that left is probably another town's gain. The loss of a business in a town that is struggling anyway probably means that a new business is going to be harder to attract. After all, towns are rated by companies that provide such ratings based on how much of a consumer market and how much of a trained labor force are available. Town leaders know they are likely to be rated too low to attract the kind of new business they want.

The loss of a business and the jobs that go with it are especially troubling both economically and culturally for a community that has worked collectively to secure the business in the first place. It may have taken a property tax write-off to attract the business. It probably took the work of the town manager, an economic development committee, public hearings, and word-of-mouth publicity to persuade the community as well as the business to come. The effort's success is a feather in the community's cap.

Alex Anderson is the CEO of the kind of business that one would be surprised to find in Findley, a sparsely settled Midwestern town of fifteen hundred, surrounded by cornfields and pastureland, three hours from the nearest city. His company specializes in polymer science applications that range from industrial components to resin transfer molding to Styrofoam recycling. The reason the company is in such a small, out-of-the-way place is that the community realized it was disintegrating back in the 1970s and got together to see if it could attract a high-tech firm that did not need to be near a city. Success came when the community persuaded the son

of one of its families to return from a city where he was working. The son recruited several of his friends and the rest was
history.

For Mr. Anderson, though, keeping the company afloat has
been a struggle. "Everything militates against it," he admits.
"It's extremely difficult to overcome the prejudice against
small towns." It's been hard to secure government contracts.
It's been equally difficult to recruit employees because people think the place is a hick town. "There's lip service in this
country to preserving small towns, but it's just lip service. It
doesn't extend in any real way toward making that possible."
The town is still disintegrating, he says. None of his grown
children live anywhere near.

People like Mr. Anderson who love their rural communities and want to preserve the small-town culture are often the
first to admit that the culture isn't in sync with what they need
to stay in business. For instance, he thinks his company's success is because he and its management team came in from the
outside. "Local people get immersed in the problems their
community is having and they can't see beyond those problems," he says, which is why having experience elsewhere is
essential. He cites as an example the fact that one of his most
effective managers lived in China, and because of that, the
company now has a branch office in Beijing.

The quandaries rural communities face in keeping businesses and providing jobs also relate directly to the "brain
drain" problem. When all the good jobs that require college
are elsewhere, the jobs that remain in small towns are unlikely
to be high-paying, plentiful, or secure. White-collar jobs are
limited. The remaining opportunities are semi-skilled jobs
in factories, if any are still present, construction, fast food,

semi-skilled healthcare, or in larger towns that require commuting. If a high-tech company happens to be in a small town, the training its employees need is likely to be lacking.

This difficulty is another one Mr. Anderson's company has faced. He says he doesn't mean to be harsh about it but kids come to him looking for employment and they have high school degrees but can hardly read and write. The ones he hires pretty much must be trained on the job. He tells them, "My motto is if you're not getting one percent better or half a percent better every day, you're automatically getting half a percent worse." His company instituted a reading program and it mostly serves to weed people out because they aren't used to the rigor it requires.

CULTURAL THREATS

Were economic and demographic problems not enough, rural communities are facing what residents view as threats to the feelings of togetherness and consensus they value. The difficulties come in different forms in different communities, sometimes from newcomers and sometimes from family rivalries that have been simmering for decades. Absent those, generational conflicts frequently pose worries about where the community's values may be headed.

A woman we talked with in Newborough, for instance, described the community as having "dual cultures." Long-time residents composed one side. They were ruggedly independent, wanted the community to be free of outside intervention, and hoped it would remain unchanged. Newcomers—which meant anyone who had arrived in the past two decades—were younger, more liberal and pluralistic in outlook, had more interests outside the community, and more often pushed for zoning and environmental regulations. The two were especially divided on climate change, the old-timers thinking it was not human-made and the newcomers thinking it was.

A cultural divide like this is not unusual, given what studies show about differences among age cohorts, and it wouldn't be particularly problematic in a rural community except for the fiction that everybody is the same. It bothers long-time residents of small communities who have worked to preserve the community's shared values to see those values changing. It may be especially worrisome if the changes are taking place among their own children.

Among the farmers I studied, generational conflict was something they talked about reluctantly, but it surfaced repeatedly in the candid interviews we conducted. Karen Meeks, for instance, explained that one of the reasons she and her husband had considered leaving Fairfield was the frustrations they experienced farming with her dad. He was used to farming on a smaller scale and if he had two tractors wanted them to be the same and to be working together in the same field. Farming on a larger scale made that impractical. He didn't keep up on the latest innovations in agronomy either, and yet vetoed any of the new ideas she and her husband proposed.

Other farm families described conflicts between wives and their mothers or mothers-in-law. In one instance the wife said she was frequently depressed because her husband seemed to prefer eating at her mother's house, which was just up the road. In another instance the mother-in-law excluded her daughter-in-law from all the important farm decisions.

Gender conflict also came up in many of the interviews we conducted among townspeople. Many of the communities were patrilocal, meaning that the son returned to his home community because of family land or a family business, bringing a wife who was a stranger to the community. The wives in these instances frequently felt ostracized or in the best scenarios found learning to fit in a lengthy process. The adjustment was particularly difficult for women whose careers were interrupted.

Judy Marsh is one of Mr. Cahill's neighbors. She and her husband have lived in Gulfdale for nearly three decades. But it's never felt like home, she says. She grew up in a city, met her husband in college, and for the first decade of their marriage they lived in a city and she taught high school chemistry. Then her husband got a job in Gulfdale. "My husband decided this is where we would live. I came because of him. It wasn't my choice! I could go on for an hour about that!" She didn't. But she made it clear that she doesn't like living where there are no decent places to shop or eat out. She misses having a career. She visits her daughter in Dallas as often as she can.

Living as they did in a small community where people gossiped, the conflicts and frustrations were usually shared more easily with distant friends and relatives than locally. But not always. Conflicts sometimes became so open that the rift dividing the community remained for years. Religion was often the source of disagreement. For instance, one community had two nearly identical Lutheran churches, the two representing an ethnic split from years ago. Many communities had churches that originated from recent theological and moral conflicts. A prominent Southern Baptist church in the center of town, for instance, would be rivaled by a new Independent Baptist church on the outskirts, and the dwindling Methodist church would be the remains of half the congregation's departure to an Assemblies of God church. In one such community, the members who stayed and the members who left were so angry they refused to speak to one another, even if they happened to be dining at the same restaurant.

The usual narrative about severe community problems bringing people together was popular; however, there were exceptions. Natural disasters sparked conflict in several instances. For example, a Midwestern town suffered a devastating tornado in the 1990s, destroying about half the residences and businesses but leaving enough of the community intact that people decided to rebuild. The trouble came when the affected and unaffected residents started seeing things differently. The one wanted to rebuild quickly, the other wanted to take more time and include a wider community makeover. Insurance claims and zoning issues complicated the issues. A decade later the two sides were still at odds.

Conventional wisdom suggests that conflicts and setbacks within tight-knit communities prompt members to seek outsiders to blame. That dynamic is present in anger toward Washington (chapter 4) and in racial and ethnic bigotry (chapter 6). That is not the whole story, however. The communities I studied were aware of the problems they faced. They talked as candidly about their community's failings as they did about its attractions. They could pinpoint the year the school closed, the reason the factory left, and why the church split. Those were regrettable events but identifiable. The harder dynamic to grasp was the perception that something about the community itself was in jeopardy.

How a family moving away or a teenager on meth becomes a *community* problem, rather than only a personal one, requires returning briefly to what I discussed in the previous chapter. These are threats—some more serious than others—to the community's moral fabric. The moral fabric is the shared notion that what the community represents is right. Things do not have to go well all the time for the community to be deeply ingrained in its members' sense of who they are. They do not think of themselves only as individuals and individual families but for better or worse as part of the collectivity in which they live. It is their common location, their shared norms of how to behave and who to respect, and their sense of obligation.

Being part of a moral community, even when it sits lightly on people's shoulders, means that sensing your community is declining and your young people are falling behind is a reflection in small measure on you. You may not be affected personally, but you are part of a failing community. The school that closes is yours. You may be well educated yourself, but you feel that people consider you a hick simply because of where you live. The stereotype in your mind says people like you lack intelligence. That stereotype is reinforced when an outsider speaks to you slowly and asks if you've ever been out of the state.

An unraveling of the moral community occurs just as well when you are happily adapting to the changes your lifestyle requires. You commute to a city to work and to a suburb to shop. You attend church there too. It offers more for your family. You enjoy visiting your siblings who years ago became city dwellers. You'd like to be more involved in local affairs but you are too busy. The occasional thread of nostalgia reminds you of how things have changed.

The problems rural people experience in their communities go a long way toward disconfirming the rosy rustic view that suggests everything in these simple places is just fine. Clearly there are reasons enough for residents to be frustrated, even angry, that things are not better than they are. We misunderstand the situation, though, if we assume these are the only reasons residents lash out so angrily when they attend political rallies. They are usually realistic about the shortcomings of their communities. They may hope to secure a new manufacturing plant but know the chances of that happening are small. The population has held steady long enough or been declining slowly enough that they don't expect the town to disappear anytime soon. It is more the almost inexpressible concern that their way of life is eroding, shifting imperceptibly under the feet, and being discredited and attacked from the outside that poses the greatest threat. As far as the immediate problems are concerned, there are makeshift solutions in place that may not be working as well as they used to but nevertheless cast additional perspective on what it means to live as a moral community.

3

Makeshift Solutions

Alexis de Tocqueville's observations about America in the 1830s could just as well pertain to much of what happens in rural communities today. The individualism that worried him even as he admired it is present in townspeople's insistence on looking out for themselves. So are the numerous voluntary associations that Tocqueville credited citizens with for solving their problems locally and thus upholding democracy instead of looking for government assistance.[1]

Rural communities are awash in such organizations. To be a respected member of the community means not only taking care of yourself and your family but also pitching in to help in small ways to address the community's problems. What has changed is that small communities are interconnected and dependent on wider resources and opportunities and constraints as never before. Working with limited effectiveness to address local problems is often as frustrating as knowing that the problems exist in the first place.

Political scientist Robert D. Putnam argued in *Bowling Alone* that Americans' engagement in their communities has fallen dramatically during the past few decades. Fewer people visit their neighbors, host their friends for dinner, hold membership in voluntary associations, and do volunteer work. The fault is ours, Putnam says, because we spend too much time at home by ourselves watching television, and, if we do join something, it's mostly by sending a check. He observes, however, that small towns and rural areas are different. They may be affected by the same trends, but they are more altruistic, honest, and trusting than other Americans. "Getting involved in community affairs is more inviting," he says, "when the scale of everyday life is smaller and more intimate."[2]

In a national survey I conducted in the late 1990s, I found that residents of small towns or rural areas were significantly more likely than residents of cities or suburbs to feel they could count on their neighbors for help if someone in their family became seriously ill. However, suburbanites were more likely than residents of small towns to hold membership in a voluntary organization, other than a church. Residents of small communities explained in interviews that voluntary organizations had sometimes shut down as population declined, more people were working and shopping outside the community, and an aging population had fewer reasons to participate in organizations for children and youth. It worried them nevertheless to see these trends. They believed that small communities could be self-sufficient if people pitched in and worked together. In the absence of that, they feared the community was losing its sense of moral order.[3]

VOLUNTEERING

Bethany Pritchard is one of the women we talked with in Fairfield. She is a college graduate in her late thirties, is married to an attorney who practices in town, and spends most of her time mothering her five children. The youngest is one and the oldest is fourteen. That means long hours each day spent cooking, cleaning, doing the shopping, paying the bills, and ferrying the children to their various activities. Part of being a mother and a church member in a small town is also doing volunteer work. She is president of the older children's swim team and a member of the school council. She also hosts a prayer group at church and delivers for Meals on Wheels. She is not atypical in these respects. She says she enjoys feeling like she is helping people outside her own family. She feels it contributes to the community. She knows too that there is an implicit expectation in the community about being involved in these ways. She sees her neighbors at the cancer walk and the annual March of Dimes event. The same is true of school functions and Meals on Wheels. She gets irritated at the "other set of people" who don't have time and don't help out "for whatever reason."

Whether people in rural communities volunteer more or at the same rates as people elsewhere, two things stand out: first, there are far more voluntary associations per capita in small communities than in larger ones; specifically, one association for every hundred people in communities under 1,000 population, one for every two hundred people in communities of 25,000, and only one for every five hundred people in communities of 100,000 or more; and second, people in rural communities attach high value to people who pitch in, giving high marks to people who volunteer and get things organized but withholding respect from people who are too busy to get involved.[4]

The desire to roll up your sleeves and get things done locally is an important aspect of small-town identity and pride.

Sometimes it doesn't amount to much—planting flowers in front of the library, clearing a vacant lot, helping with the annual pancake breakfast. Nevertheless, people say they feel good about themselves when they do something for the town.

"Have you ever seen a Norman Rockwell calendar? That's my town." This was Jake Stansworth talking about his community, Stuart Bluffs, a town of a thousand on the Northern Plains. The town was founded in the 1870s shortly after the U.S. Cavalry drove out the Pawnees and a railroad company secured rights to much of the land. Mr. Stansworth is in his seventies now, retired from having worked for the gas company and later as a heating and air conditioning repairman. "You've got to take on your responsibilities, be involved in the community to make things work," he says. He's put in his time on the Chamber of Commerce, the Lions Club, and on committees at his church. The town had more people in 1910 than it does today, but the tall brick buildings that went up in the 1890s on both sides of Main Street are well tended. Mr. Stansworth personally renovated two of them. "Kept them from falling in," he says. "I'm very proud of those accomplishments."

Like other places, the community groups in small towns are as much about schmoozing as working on projects. Most any day there's a group at the church or the Legion hall. It helps that people in their eighties still feel it's safe to get out and drive. They mean it when they say things in small towns move at a slower pace. But this is also the kind of networking that gets things done. Next thing the town council knows they've suggested starting a fitness center or opening a laundromat. The drawback, though, is that the Old-timers Coffee Club is just as likely to be the ones opposing efforts to start something new.

The formal organizations that are tasked with getting community work done are more likely to be Kiwanis, Lions, the Chamber of Commerce, the VFW, and special-purpose committees, such as the hospital board, the library board, and the school board. The efforts benefit from the fact that the gentry in small towns are expected to take—and generally do take—leadership roles. Mr. Cahill's participation on the town council in Gulfdale is an example, as is Mr. Somers's presidency of Newborough's Chamber of Commerce. To be sure, many of these organizations are national franchises that follow the same procedures wherever they are located. In small towns, however, the same people meet week after week and get to know each other. They get to initiate local projects that give them a sense of empowerment in the community. And they can do things their own way per what they believe best suits the community. Newborough's civic groups, for example, recently built a new library, but instead of constructing a new building, they renovated an old house. "It's like it belongs in the town," one of the planners observed.

But rural communities are increasingly faced with the reality that getting anything done requires participating in state and regional organizations. Fairfield farmer John Meeks, for example, participates in Farm Bureau, the state wheat growers' association, and the regional watershed advisory task force. These organizations connect small places with large interest groups, but people like Meeks worry that their voice is weak compared to large corporate agribusiness enterprises (such as Monsanto and ConAgra) and environmentalist groups.

Many towns, I learned, have spawned so many volunteer organizations over the years that with changing populations and political realities these groups wind up competing for scarce resources instead of truly representing the community's best interests. Newborough, for instance, basically had to do an end-run around its many volunteer groups by initiating a new organization called Four Sectors—schools, county government, farmers, and business—that picked a few projects and tried to persuade the state to fund them.

Although Newborough experienced some success, other towns of similar size were frustrated by not knowing who in state government to contact or knowing that making contact was close to hopeless because of tight state budgets. Writing formal grant proposals with little experience to draw on and dealing with the accompanying regulations and accountability requirements was challenging as well.

The resulting difficulty that many of the town managers in the communities I studied expressed was the local citizenry complaining that nothing was being done to address their problems. Sheila Ankerholz, for instance, is the town manager in an East Coast community of twenty thousand that by most indications is doing better than its neighbors. However, the community recently lost one of its long-term manufacturing plants and many of the residents are under-employed, working at part-time jobs, or commuting 30 miles to jobs in a city. People are angry and afraid.

"We have a lot of screamers," she says. "What they're yelling about may be completely unreasonable, but they have a need to vent." So they show up at town meetings or they come to her. "Once you blow through all the smoke, a lot of times it's a problem that isn't possible to address at this level. It's very hard for people to understand that. You can give them the reasons but they are taxpayers and feel that somebody should fix things."

ECONOMIC DEVELOPMENT

The challenge that brings small-town culture most sharply into juxtaposition with the hard realities of community survival is the quest for jobs. The principal responsibility for efforts in rural communities of any size is usually a committee headed by a salaried or volunteer specialist whose job it is to scout local markets, keep tabs on economic opportunities, participate in regional planning meetings, and secure grants.

The development officers we talked with were to a person frustrated. They may have had a few successes in keeping jobs from leaving or bringing in new ones and those accomplishments earned them praise in the community. However, it was nearly impossible to achieve anything truly ambitious. Being located too far from a city, not having an interstate highway nearby, and being the small kid on the block among larger players were usually recipes for failure.

In one of the fishing villages we studied we talked with a city manager—he explained that "city manager" was a legal term lest we think he was putting on airs to call a town of nine thousand a city—who articulated clearly why economic development in small towns often misfires even when it succeeds. Tom French was finishing his fifteen-year term as city manager when we talked with him. He was raised here, said to hell with the "brain drain," and left when he was eighteen to experience life in the big city. Twenty-five years later he returned. He knows the community's history, knows when it transitioned from shipping to boat building to fishing, and understands that its economic survival depends on changing with the times.

The rub, as he sees it, is that economic development has become the preserve of economists who think they know best. "Oh, we don't care what you think," they say, "this is what you should do." That was who he listened to before he returned to his hometown. He could mark off a number of success stories in his previous jobs. But then one day he woke up and said, "Who am I doing this for?"

"I realized that the community was better off except that everyone had moved somewhere else." He told the people in his hometown, "We have to be careful what we wish for, because if growing the economy here means that all the people here leave and other people come in and enjoy it, we've failed."

The approach he favors is "bottom up." He calls it "politically incorrect" because it assumes ordinary citizens know best, whereas politicians are usually in it for themselves.

"Bottom up" doesn't mean convening a committee, either. The trouble with that, he says, is that the people who have time to be on a committee aren't the ones you want. You want the ones who are too busy because they are being productive at what they do.

"What I do is come up with an idea that I think might be a good idea. Then I go over to your house and chat about it and I digest what you say. Then I go over to the grocery store and talk to that guy and then down to the local garage. I come back and digest it all, rework it into something more palatable, and go back around again. Maybe several times until I think I have a consensus. Then I go out and say, 'Hey guys, it looks like you guys have a great idea here. Yes, let's do it.'"

Mr. French's approach was basically an acknowledgment of the particularities of small-town culture. People want to feel they have a say in community decisions. They are like pieces in a puzzle that isn't complete without every piece. They live in the same place and yet have different perspectives that need to be considered, all within the framework of the community's natural and human resources.

There is reason for caution in small-town views like Mr. French's, though. Keeping things local by iteratively talking to the grocer and the garage man and their neighbors is, as Mr. French says, the "politically incorrect" way to do things. It takes time and mostly ignores specialized technical expertise. It is distrustful of politicians, especially those running the federal government. "Are we going to be able to continue what we're doing," he wonders, "or is the federal government going to cripple us?"

"We've gone from being a battered and bewildered feeling-sorry-for-ourselves community to a vibrant one that's going to take care of ourselves," he says. "The government can help us, but it better keep out of our way!"

The frustration with politicians and government that town leaders like Mr. French express is not so much fear of being stymied in pursuing local aspirations. It is, rather, knowing that the community is far less self-sustaining than they would like to think it is. As much as they may disdain external experts and governmental entities, they know the community is dependent on them, just as it increasingly is on national and international markets.

HELPING THE NEEDY

While rural communities tackle the big long-term issues of attracting businesses and anticipating large-scale economic transitions, the 10 percent or so who are unemployed and the 20 percent or so who are under-employed and needing assistance are the immediate challenges that require makeshift solutions. Small towns manage the problem through private charity when the number of needy people is small. An indigent widow or a bedridden farmer could usually count on neighborly assistance if they were well-known in the community. In many instances, private charity also extended to people who otherwise were "them," at least if there weren't too many and if they demonstrated gratitude by getting a job and joining a local church. Donations and volunteer efforts at a community center that serves free meals and provides shelter, or a deacon's fund that quietly helps a family keep its heat and electricity running, were common. And talk of distrusting the government did not prevent participation in regional food banks and public welfare programs.

The small-town tradition of volunteers helping the needy naturally falls short when the demographics change and the needs increase—a problem exacerbated when younger people move away, leaving an aging population behind. Gulfdale's Reverend Simpson, for instance, told us that two men from his church volunteer four hours twice a week to help the needy. They helped five hundred families the past year. He wonders how they did it and wishes there were more volunteers. Another man drives up from the coast occasionally and screens people who need jobs. But many of the people he screens are unable to work. Countywide, one of every ten otherwise employable residents is disabled.

The situation was much the same in Newborough. One of the pastors we spoke with participates in the community's council on aging, which he says is struggling to keep up with local needs. Another church maintains a house for the disabled, and volunteers help neighbors who cannot drive to the doctor. But disability has left tens of thousands of rural residents nationwide unable to work, especially when the only available jobs require long commutes and are physically demanding.[5]

Never far from the stories townspeople tell of helping the needy, though, is the question of who is truly needy and who is gaming the system. In places where taking responsibility for yourself is the norm, suspicion is often present toward the disabled and unemployed. Richard Pruitt heads a committee in Fairfield charged with locating jobs and training people to fill them. In that capacity, he feels it is his responsibility to do all he can to help those less fortunate than he is. He says it isn't just a matter of his job to help. "It's just part of my moral upbringing to take it personally if I can't do that." The same sense of moral responsibility he feels about himself, though, pertains to the people he tries to help. "There's got to be a safety net," he says, referring to government programs. "However, there's a fine line between people who can't work and people who don't want to work." And that being the case, he thinks the more you can do to help without government being involved, the better it is. The reason is that hands-on programs can take a more personal approach. At least he hopes so.

The hands-on approach nevertheless usually requires money to be effective and, increasingly, the money is not there unless local taxes are increased or outside funds can be secured. Outside funds are granted on a competitive basis, which means one community finds it awkward to ask another community for advice, and to complicate things, demands for greater accountability to state and federal agencies require more time and skill at grant writing and reporting than the official staffing a small agency in a small town can justify. To make matters worse, the partisanship that has overtaken state and federal bureaus means having to play politics to have any chance of receiving support.

Never content simply to look problems in the eye and accept them as givens, rural people are also quick to blame themselves for not trying harder. Mr. Somers, for example, frets that Newborough is falling behind because the community is looking too much for outside help, such as appealing to the state for funds or going to other towns for healthcare and assistance for the elderly. "In rural communities we don't have all the services right next door, so we rely on other places," he says. "I don't mean to sound isolationist, but I think we should pay more attention to our own Main Street. At least that was the old model. I think we'd be better off if we expected more of ourselves."

These are the difficulties that add to the sense of small towns being beleaguered. The problems are too big to handle alone, even though communities would like to be self-sufficient. Citizens want more and often contribute less in terms of volunteer time. Getting things done is less a function of local control. Rural communities have never been fully in charge of their own destinies, but the people who live in them now have reason to feel they are even less in control than in the past.

If rural people are susceptible to appeals that blame others—Washington, minorities, immigrants—for their problems, we must recognize clearly the psychological toll that seemingly insurmountable problems take on rural people themselves. The interviews we conducted were interrupted frequently by people pausing to get a grip on their emotions as they described goals they knew they would never achieve and the attendant frustrations. They were on the whole content with the knowledge that life was what it was, whether that meant having given up a career, suffering from job loss or the failure of a farm, or growing old without children nearby.

One of the farmers I discussed in my book *In the Blood* talked animatedly in response to my questions, but at the end of the interview said he had something more to say. He said a few years ago he was so depressed that he wished more than anything to die. He made it through. Another farmer I got to know committed suicide.[6]

RELIGION

Like many Americans in larger communities, the setbacks rural people experience, they said, are manageable because of their faith in God. Herb and Linda Tobias, a couple in their fifties who operate a thousand- acre, third-generation corn and soybean farm in the Midwest, are typical in this regard. Any Sunday morning finds them at the Baptist church in McClelland, a town about 12 miles from their farm. The trees here struggle against the hot, dry wind that blows in the summer, and most of the houses are modest single-story dwellings that also appear to be hunkering down. The Baptist church, built in the 1980s with an expansive fellowship hall and educational wing, is a large brick cathedral-roofed structure that would make any community proud. Mr. and Mrs. Tobias nevertheless admit to being disgruntled because it's been hard for their small community to attract good preachers and the one who came last year leaves them shaking their heads sometimes. But they feel it is God more than the church that gets them through rough times.

"We were just about out of debt a few years ago," Mrs. Tobias says. "We thought maybe we could buy some new machinery, but then the crop failed that year and we were back in debt again."

Mr. Tobias chips in, "Everybody at church was angry and upset too. Nobody was getting out of debt and we were thinking we'd have to let the pastor go and maybe shut down the church. Besides that, my mother took sick and died and my dad needed a lot of care. It was just like there were mountains of things to worry about. Linda and I weren't sure we'd get through it. But we did. Somehow God gave us the strength."

Hearing people in small towns talking about their faith, I couldn't help wondering if they might be a bit superstitious. Did they think rain would come if they prayed for it? Did they give money to their church in hopes that God would bless their crops?

Nobody admitted to it if that was what they thought. It was rather that, on top of the usual uncertainties of life—illness, accidents, bereavement—they also faced the uncertainties of bad weather, crop failures, and market fluctuations that could bankrupt an otherwise prudent farmer or the shopkeepers in town who depended on farmers.

Faith wasn't a quick fix for their family's finances or the town's economy. An outsider would probably say its role was mostly therapeutic. It kept them from being as depressed as they would have been otherwise. When times were tough, it helped them take a longer-term perspective, sometimes steeling their resolve to stick with what they were doing.

I came away thinking, too, that faith was perhaps more meaningful in small towns because few other options were available. It wasn't going to do much good to send letters to the governor in hopes of getting a new fiscal plan that would help. The nearest psychiatrist was probably an hour away and the best local alternative might be drugs or alcohol.

This thought about small towns grew on me after stopping for gas one day in the middle of nowhere. I was traveling one of those coast-to-coast highways writers like to take when they send missives about the heartland to city newspapers. I doubted if any of those writers had stopped here. Besides the filling station, there was a small brick church and a large, towering grain elevator. Nothing else. The reason I stopped was that I knew something special had happened in this place a couple of years earlier.

A filmmaker who had relatives nearby had made a documentary about the community's struggles. In one scene, the camera pans the humble living room of a farm woman as she talks about her life. Mid-scene, as you begin to hear noise in the background, the woman walks to the front door, stands on the porch, and watches helplessly as a massive hailstorm wipes out her income for the coming year. In another scene, a small group of four or five young men are talking at the grain elevator. They talk about drinking and drugs and they talk about trying to stop and finding help by going to church.[7]

By the time I stopped for gas a couple of years later, I learned that the church had ceased having services and the grain elevator was now operated by computer from a larger town. I wondered about the faith that maybe was still there among the scattered farmhouses that remained. Rural religion is stereotypically known to have a kind of Bible-belt theology that pits evil and good sharply against one another. Drugs and church. Hailstorms and harvest. Despair and hope. It was not hard to see how the theology made sense.

4

Washington's Broken

Rural America's dissatisfaction with Washington had been simmering for a long time. Rural voters were grateful to Franklin Delano Roosevelt for saving them from the Depression, but not as grateful as later renditions would often suggest. They especially didn't like the Agricultural Adjustment Act and FDR's efforts to pack the Supreme Court. Eisenhower was their man, yet farmers in his own state disliked his farm policies. Nixon embarrassed them for having supported him and Carter disappointed them. They agreed with Reagan that "government is not the answer; government is the problem."

Although rural voters mostly supported George W. Bush in 2000 and again in 2004, many of the ones I talked with in 2007 and 2008 had grown weary of the Iraq War and were displeased that little had been done to cut the deficit or curb abortion. It was probably not surprising that they felt little affinity for Barack Obama, not only because of his race but also because he was the only president since Kennedy (other than George H. W. Bush) who did nothing to embellish his image as a person with small-town and agrarian roots. They liked John McCain because he was a war hero and Sarah

Palin because she presented herself as a person from a small town who spoke for grassroots America.

In the communities I studied, voters' remarks about the federal government were among the most vehement of any topic we discussed. There was occasional animosity toward the town manager or mayor. Local officials usually received at least passing marks, though, as long as they were insiders who understood the community norms. Governors and state legislators drew mixed responses. Governors who kept taxes from increasing and representatives who visited the community from time to time generally received positive comments; others did not. The federal government was different. It was distant, yet intrusive, professionalized, yet lacking in common sense.

To someone following political headlines, it would probably seem obvious that rural voters are upset with Washington for failing to lower the local joblessness rate and reduce taxes. A different picture emerges when you listen to local narratives. Small communities have stories about their history that help make sense of the present. The story Gulfdale's majority-white population knows by heart is the federal government's intrusion on their lives during Reconstruction. They don't say much about what preceded Reconstruction or what happened when it ended, although some of the old-timers remember voting for Goldwater in 1964 when LBJ pressed desegregation. Fairfield's story says its early settlers came to America to escape government repression in Europe and their descendants have been skeptical of big government ever since. Newborough's tells of fighting for the Union during the Civil War, which, oddly for a New England town, includes a backstory of half the town's residents favoring the South's claim of state's rights against the federal government.

Down the street, a block from the courthouse in Gulfdale, Reverend Ralph Patterson officiates over the largest Protestant church in town. Most Sundays the sanctuary is nearly full for both the nine o'clock and eleven o'clock services. People here take their religion seriously. Reverend Patterson is a native of the state and knows the community well. His take on local affairs is genuinely appreciative. He speaks with quiet pride about the slow-paced way of life, feeling safe, and people helping one another. Recently assisting a family of three whose breadwinner lost his job, he says, illustrates how people are playing their expected role in God's kingdom. "It's a wonderful experience," he observes. When you see others helping and being helped. "It just transcends the moment into something that's bigger than us."

But Reverend Patterson's tone shifts when his comments turn to Washington. What would it take for things in the community to really get better? "Get some new leadership in Washington!" He pauses as he realizes the question wasn't meant to be about politics, but continues. "People up there in Washington, doesn't matter what party it is, those people don't know a thing about what's going on down here in Gulfdale. They don't want to listen to us. They don't care!"

All they care about, he says, is their special interest groups and getting reelected. "Our people would love to go down there and just make a clean sweep!" he exclaims. "Only put people in Washington with some common sense." If common sense is what people in Gulfdale live by, he doesn't understand why the federal government can't do things the same way.

And that reminds him of what else the people of Gulfdale hate about Washington. "Those people up there in Washington, they think they know more than we do. They treat us like second-class citizens, like we're dumb hicks, like we don't know what's going on."

It was almost as if Reverend Patterson foresaw the 2016 election. He declares, "I think they're going to have a rude awakening up there in Washington in the next few years. People are just fed up. They want to put some other people up there that's got some common sense."

WASHINGTON IS DISTANT

The most common refrain in rural people's criticisms of Washington parallels Reverend Patterson's remarks. Washington is distant from their communities, geographically and culturally. As far as they can see, the federal government hasn't the least interest in trying to understand rural communities' problems, let alone do anything to fix them. The sentiment is so pervasive, so vehement, that it is hard to get underneath it to see what it means. And yet it is clearly more than a knee-jerk reaction. It bears a close affinity with the threads that tie together rural communities' accepted way of life. Washington stands for everything causing these threads to unravel.

The basis of small-town life is not only that it is "rural" but that it is small, which means what happens is close enough to witness firsthand and to experience intimately enough to understand and have some hope of influencing. Whether Washington was "up there," "down there," or someplace else in people's minds, it was so far away that people we talked with couldn't understand it—"so distant that I just feel helpless." And they were pretty sure Washington didn't understand them. "They're just not listening to us out here."

Whoever Washington was listening to, it wasn't anybody "small." Not the small farmer, the small-business owner, or people living in small places. It was somebody "big." It was the big interests, big cities, big businesses, and big farmers. Washington itself was big, too big to get anything done, run by the big boys who only knew how to talk big. It was "a bunch of big-headed guys" there with brilliant ideas that didn't work. Washington was doing everything it could either to bail out or regulate big banks, but in the meantime small banks were hurting. Washington was catering to corporate farming interests and lobbyists instead of small farmers. "Remember the little man" was a frequent plea.

Washington's perceived remoteness from rural areas is reminiscent of decades-old perceptions of rural-urban differences. By the end of the nineteenth century the agrarian ideal that had inspired Jefferson had become in many urban depictions the last vestige of a rough-hewn but ignorant population hoping to flee from the farms to a better life in the cities. Rural people could argue that the cities teemed with gangsters and hucksters—that it was the "country mouse" against the "city slicker"—but it was they who lacked and coveted electric lights and indoor plumbing. It was they whom the twentieth century would read about as H. L. Mencken's "simian peasants" and Richard Hofstadter's "paranoid style."[1]

Rural voters' view that Washington is beholden to urban interests surfaced frequently in my interviews. "Don't forget us," one rural Midwesterner pleaded. "Maybe our population isn't as big as cities, but we represent something cities never will." Said another, "Don't just focus on your urban areas, which I realize is where the money is. Focus on your rural areas where you still have strong morals and values." These concerns, however, reflect twenty-first-century realities as well as time-worn misgivings. For example, when pushed to say what they meant by urban interests, the typical response was about the Obama administration bailing out Wall Street and General Motors.

The contrast in views about "Washington" and "cities" was in fact significant. Cities were certainly perceived as fundamentally different from small towns. It was hard to find your way around in cities, easier to be victimized by crime, and difficult to hold onto the belief that everyone was the same. However, cities were not an unknown. Many of the small-town people we talked to had vacationed in cities, done business in cities, and knew people who lived in cities. They were proud that a son or daughter or a neighbor's son or daughter who lived in a city was doing well. Many had siblings who lived in cities. Nor were cities un-appreciated. They were fun places to have visited and to talk about having visited. People in cities might need schooling on what was of value in small towns. But none of the rural people we talked to claimed that rural communities were somehow the "real America."

Views of cities rarely evoked negative comments about wealthy people, even though it was obvious that wealthy people often lived in cities. The occasional critical remark was about a wealthy person they knew in their own community who put on airs. Otherwise, comments about wealthy people were generally favorable, reflecting the view that rich farmers, business owners, and doctors who lived in their communities had earned their money by working hard, treated other people fairly, and did their share and more to support community organizations. In these respects, views differed significantly from the rural complaints articulated by populists in the 1890s whose criticisms focused on railroad barons charging exploitative transportation fees and East Coast bankers charging exorbitant interest rates on farm loans. The lives of rural people we talked with were rarely connected to wealthy people in coastal cities in these ways.

WASHINGTON IS INTRUSIVE

The difference with Washington was that it was not only big and distant but was also perceived to be intervening in small communities in ways that were threatening. This view was best paraphrased in the statement that Washington wouldn't be so bad if it would just "leave us alone." But Washington was not leaving them alone. It was in their collective lives when they needed money for the school or a renovation project. It was in their personal lives with regulations and taxes.

Town managers, mayors, and members of town councils most often saw Washington intruding in community affairs through unfunded mandates. One community's leaders were upset because they were required to install a new sewage treatment plant to meet federal regulations. Another town was in danger of losing its hospital, leaders claimed, because of new standards. Other complaints focused on emergency preparedness and accommodations for the physically challenged.

"You start dumping on us with all these mandates," a town manager in an East Coast community of five thousand explained, "and it gets very difficult. We just don't have the money." He continued, "If we have to do it, it means the things that are really affecting people, like the police, the parks, trash collection, and the schools, are the things that get cut. It's very frustrating." The concern was not that these federal mandates were necessarily bad ideas, only that the towns' budgets were already stretched. If funding was available, town leaders were happy to comply.

That was less true of people who had been mobilized by the Tea Party. To them the federal government's actions were not only intrusive but also unconstitutional. As an activist in one of the Southwestern states explained, "We want local people to be in control instead of the federal government. We need to get back to what the Constitution says. The federal government is involved in a lot of stuff the Constitution has nothing to do with. We just shouldn't be in some of the stuff we're in. It ought to be local people and the states who handle it."

The more typical, non-activist residents' complaints usually focused on taxes. There was a sense—probably shared by taxpayers everywhere—that taxes were too high. The additional complaint was that tax money was being drained from small towns to subsidize projects that did not help small towns. This was the grievance about bailouts helping Wall Street and General Motors. As a woman in a small Southern town remarked, "The large corporations get tax breaks and the small communities have to pay for them." It was a complaint that surfaced in criticisms of urban renewal and housing projects as well. As often as not, though, the concerns were unspecified. It was just that Washington was telling people what to do without knowing anything about them.

Farmers were far more informed than the average townsperson in this regard. Farmers' livelihoods were directly influenced by government agricultural policies. They also had a significant influence in many of the communities we studied.

Besides their role in the local economy, they shaped public opinion, often by serving on county boards, and in the case of semi-retired farmers and farmers with time on their hands during off seasons, this took place at the local coffee shop. One view was that government should simply get out of farmers' lives. "Keep your fingers out and let me do as I please," said one in the upper Great Plains. Said another, "Get out of my way and let me do the best job I can do on my own."

The emotion in comments such as "back off!" "get off my back!" and "get out of our life!" reflected years of frustration in which farmers felt like pawns being manipulated by trade policies and programs aimed at curbing supply one year and promoting it the next. It sometimes reflected what farmers said was an inferiority complex rooted in feeling that people looked down on them for living in the country and doing manual labor. They figured they were just as intelligent as anyone else and kept up with the latest information about agronomy, animal husbandry, and the environment. As one woman declared, "Don't assume I'm stupid and don't know anything just because I'm a farmer!" Many of them farmed with equipment costing hundreds of thousands of dollars. They felt the government was trying to second-guess their decisions instead of taking their agricultural knowledge into account. Said one, "Doctors say to government get out of my way and let me practice medicine; that's what I say too."

But farmers also offered some of the most judicious thoughts about Washington. Having to report every acre they planted each year to the tenth of an acre and every bushel they harvested to the tenth of a bushel, they were keenly aware that government was part of their lives whether they wanted it to be or not. Like business operators in town, their taxes reflected profits and losses based on fuel prices, labor costs, capital gains, and depreciation. They calculated net income based on international projections and by participating in futures markets. They knew how much their annual revenue could vary because of weather alone. Nearly all the farmers we spoke with, whether they were engaged in producing wheat or corn, soybeans or cotton, or dairy products or fruits and vegetables, thought government-subsidized crop insurance was necessary. It not only kept farmers in business but also helped stabilize consumer prices from year to year.

Farmers' views of environmental regulations were less uniform. On the one hand, they generally agreed that climate change was a human-made problem that needed to be addressed. They saw the effects of climate change on their own farms, realized that fossil-fuel prices were likely to continue rising, and knew of neighbors who were experimenting—or were experimenting themselves—with solar energy and with energy-reducing, moisture-sustaining methods of tillage. They mostly agreed that regulations were needed to keep food pure, to monitor and restrict genetic engineering, and to control the influx of foreign commodities.

On the other hand, they worried that across-the-board regulations were making it harder for small farmers to stay in business. A large corporate farm operation could hire lobbyists to weigh in on expensive, genetically modified seed production and pesticides. A corporate farm could also hire attorneys to challenge regulations about chemicals, runoff from cattle pens, and water usage. A small farmer couldn't. Even the bookkeeping was becoming increasingly burdensome, they argued.

A farmer near Gulfdale offered an apt summary of the situation. "I just want to have more freedom," he said, "but I don't know how to get that." He knew the problem wasn't just the federal government telling him what to do. It was the global economy. It was Europe and Brazil and China. "I'm patriotic," he said. "As a nation we should control our own destiny. I don't like being controlled by other nations."

If it seemed from their comments that farmers and townspeople were just grousing while making no efforts to become better informed about the laws they didn't like and how to work within them, that wasn't entirely true. The farmers we talked to included ones who served on state and regional boards and in a couple of instances had been members of delegations that traveled with policy makers to the Middle East and Latin America. Even small farmers were surprisingly knowledgeable about specific federal agricultural regulations.

Town officials varied considerably in this regard. As a rule, salaried town managers were better informed and understood more clearly that they needed to be well-informed than elected mayors and council persons did. In fact, town managers were among the most frustrated people we talked with, but their pique was often directed at the ignorance of people in their communities rather than Washington.

Allison McBride, the town manager of a town in California with just under six thousand people, had plenty to say about the number of state and federal regulations that made her job difficult, but it was one of the community-minded citizens that frustrated her the most. He was part of an angry, vocal group that complained about nothing ever getting done, so when it came time for the town to apply for a federal grant, he volunteered. Frustrated with paperwork that was new to him, he called Washington and, Ms. McBride recalled, "started raising hell." A few days later Ms. McBride received a call from Washington. "We really don't think we're interested in funding anything in your town right now," the caller said.

WASHINGTON LACKS COMMON SENSE

If it were just that rural people don't like regulations and high taxes, it would be hard to understand why they think Washington is broken and how that relates to the moral fabric of their communities. The answer lies in the culture they think dominates Washington and the threat it poses to what they value about their communities. Washington's cultural distance from rural communities implies that it functions as a massive bureaucracy imposing one-size-fits-all rules on everyone without bothering to hear what ordinary people say or to understand local needs and differences. Gulfdale's town councilman Mr. Cahill thought the problem was mostly bureaucrats not dealing with issues on a "personal, hands-on" basis, like he does. "It's not because [officials] are incompetent," another town council member we talked with explained. "It's difficult to do these things remotely." How things are done in one place, he felt, is often radically different than in another place.

If the bureaucracy somehow was capable of functioning well, the concern among rural residents remains that bureaucracy in its very nature is inimical to good government. Instead of it being orderly and efficient, it appears to be chaotic and inefficient. President Obama "losing his way," as one person remarked, evoked an image of a person confused, wandering through long hallways searching for someone, anyone, with an answer.

The language rural people use to characterize Washington's brokenness also alleges that it lacks common sense. "Where in the heck do they come up with some of these ideas?" one frustrated person exclaimed. "Five hundred pages of legislation for the Army to buy lettuce," said another. "It's bullshit. That's why people are angry."

"Common sense" is the default from which rural people think Washington deviates in numerous ways. Common sense means behaving as other people do and thus being trustworthy. It implies common knowledge that any thoughtful person would understand, not esoteric specialized knowledge that only a few can possibly fathom. Lacking it can signify personal "dysfunction," as a Midwestern Republican activist put it, which causes the government to end up being dysfunctional. It also reflects the widespread view that Washington's petty politics and money-grubbing have caused it to lose touch with common people.

"I love our country, God knows I do," a rural Texan declared, but nobody in Washington struck him as having any common sense. "It's a money-hungry, dog-eat-dog place. Lobbyists are ruining it and it's just gone to pot. We just need somebody with a little gumption. Somebody to go up there and do what a common man knows to do. That's all we need!"

Washington's lack of common sense, others we spoke with suggested, is especially evident in its wastefulness. This is the cultural complaint under the surface concern about taxes. Reverend Patterson, for instance, equates common sense with being responsible about money the way he tells his parishioners to be. "We have to manage our home lives, our family budgets," he asserts. "When times get tough, we tighten up the belt. We save money. The idea up there in Washington is spend money even if you don't have it. People are sick of it!"

If Washington is not responsible about money, many of the people we spoke with also thought Washington was to blame for some of the families in their own community not being responsible with money. Maybe you could be sympathetic to indigent people in your community if you figured they were poor despite working hard. But you were less likely to be sympathetic if you thought government handouts were the problem. Consider how a man in Fairfield who rents housing to low-income families describes his tenants. He says they are struggling because the minimum wages they earn at McDonald's or Walmart don't cover the rising prices of gas for their car and medical bills for their families. Things have gotten worse, he says. And yet he blames the government for having "given them a lot of things." They "expect it now" that they have food stamps and rent subsidies. They don't seem to care like they used to. Government "handouts" have affected them to the point that they "sit home and do nothing."

This man's criticism of the poor was at least mixed with sympathy, perhaps because he was one of Fairfield's wealthier citizens and could afford to recognize that people were struggling. That was not the case of another Fairfield citizen who held a low-paying job at one of the local manufacturing plants. "Make those welfare moms get up and get a job instead of us paying for them," he declared when asked about Washington, adding, "Make *them* get up and do something. *We* work our butts off. It's just too easy for them to get free handouts."

Besides Washington lacking common sense, people said, another problem was that it wasn't getting anything done. Part of the rural ethic, they thought, was being practical. Maybe you couldn't earn more money but you made do with what you had. You patched the roof, repaired the car, and made the tractor last another year. You didn't necessarily like the mayor but you voted for him anyway because he got things done. Or you formed a local committee, as one of the town leaders in Newborough explained, and things got done because people knew each other, cared about the community's well-being, and set aside their ideologies and posturing. Washington was different—"sick." Republicans and Democrats alike said no meaningful legislation was going to be passed. The system was "broken." Both sides were "corrupt."

Perhaps it was their inferiority complex coming through, but many of the rural people we talked with also felt that the government telling them what to do was a mark of disrespect. They interpreted government policies that infringed on their lives as further evidence of being looked down on. They wanted to be viewed differently, not as being better than anyone else but as being just as good. A resident of one of the villages near Newborough put it eloquently:

> I'm a good person and my brothers and sisters are good people. We raise our families, we go to church, we support our schools, we support Boy Scouts and 4-H Clubs, and we do our business locally. We protect the environment, we improve the environment, we are environmentalists. We are socially conscious and we are hardworking businesspeople who employ people. We believe in this country!

Why any of what Washington does or how it is viewed should be a threat to rural communities stems from the fact that Washington is understandably seen as a powerful influence on the nation's culture. Its influence is not unstoppable, as they see it, at least if rural voters had allies in suburbs and cities who felt as they do. That would achieve the dramatic transformation they hope could occur in politics. They know, for their part, that they are a minority. They feel beleaguered by the changes they see in their own communities and by their sense of help-lessness on the national stage. They hope that Washington is not irreparably broken but fear that it might be.

And when it comes time to vote, they know this is how they can show Washington in a small way what they think. A man in a town of six thousand was almost giddy anticipating the next election. "There's a lot of anger and frustration here," he said. "We're going to show some folks how unhappy we are."

MORAL OUTRAGE

It is of course apparent that part of the moral outrage in rural America is driven by the conservative media they find appeal-ing because it speaks to their frustration. Concerns about wastefulness, taxes, and deficits are frequent topics of con-versation at the coffee shop more often than they probably would be otherwise because of conservative punditry on talk radio and television. The terms in which these arguments are cast matter, too, and are not strictly economic. Washington represents an affront to the moral obligations rural people be-lieve are not only right and good but also sensible. Washing-ton is a threat because it is big and powerful and because its way of thinking is fundamentally alien. Besides that, people who believe in common sense try to figure things out. There may be towns in which the Hatfields and McCoys have been feuding for years, but to people in small communities it usually seems better to work things out. After all, you probably see them often enough around town that it would be awkward if you didn't. Politicians in contrast seem to be at each other's throats about everything. Maybe you believe Republicans more than you do Democrats, but both sides seem to twist everything they say to the point that it's hard to trust anyone. And that's maddening.

I've called rural people's anger toward Washington "moral outrage" because they view the federal government's basic mode of action in recent years as an affront to their way of life. The contrasts could not be clearer, and they do not focus only on a single issue or policy. Rural communities are close, personal; Washington is distant, impersonal. People in rural places care about one another and share common understandings; people in Washington don't care and don't understand the common person; rural people know when to help and when to leave people alone; Washington intrudes unhelpfully in people's lives; rural communities are practical and use common sense; Washington's ideas are impractical and defy common sense. It was this perception of a disturbing cultural divide that prompted people again and again to say that Washington being broken was one of the most serious moral problems the country faces.

The anger toward specific policies and officeholders is nested within this larger sense of Washington being at odds with the moral communities in which people live. Deficit spending is contrary to ordinary people living within their means. Government wastefulness is the antipathy of hometown thrift. Catering to the interests of big business and cities runs counter to focusing on small places. To be "moral" in these respects is to do what is unquestionably right because it simply makes sense and to not be "moral" is to behave in fundamentally different ways.

This understanding of what it means to uphold or threaten a community's way of life differs from how an individual's morality or immorality might be regarded. People in rural communities are no more accepting than anyone else of someone who lies, cheats, steals, and commits adultery. If anything, they are more likely to condemn such acts. However, some of these individual acts reflect on the community and others do not. It all depends on how the community interprets the act. A local teen getting drunk, for example, can be interpreted as something that teens just do or that the family has problems; a spate of teen drunkenness is more likely to be understood as a community problem. So it is with public officials. Townspeople can be surprisingly indifferent to an official's sexual indiscretions as long as they seem not to be a threat to the community. They can be surprisingly unforgiving if indiscretions are interpreted differently.

A further caveat in interpreting the rancor in rural communities toward Washington is that, although they wish Washington would get out of their lives, they aren't so naïve as to think that will happen—or if it did, that nothing would be lost. Thinking that rural people are as simple-minded as that plays into the narrative that they are ignorant. They clearly are not. They understand that government is necessary to implement effective economic policies and they understand that Social Security, welfare programs, farm subsidies, and block grants help their communities. Their outrage is not only frustration toward Washington; it is also ambivalence about the role of government. A way of life that is no longer as self-sufficient as they thought it was feels like a loss of control over their own communities, even if the loss is necessary.

There is truth, then, in interpretations of rural America that say it is angry at Washington because it feels left out and left behind. The outrage is there in families and in conversations at the farmers' co-op. If it were strictly about economic issues, it would respond to policy proposals about bringing jobs and raising wages. But it is more about a perceived cultural threat that is often ill-defined even though it runs deep. A threat of this kind responds to symbolism and rituals, to feisty rhetoric and rallies.

Whether this kind of moral outrage is capable of mobilizing people into an organized populist movement, as some analysts have suggested, depends on other things. The populism of the 1890s occurred at a time when the nation was far more rural than it is today. Its strength grew in local communities to achieve reforms in state-level politics and to elevate William Jennings Bryan as the "Great Commoner" speaking for the common person. Its achievements never quite produced the large-scale reforms its proponents wanted. The populism of today has mobilized rural voters to attend rallies and to cast their votes, not for a "commoner" but for an "outsider."

The question of mobilization does reopen speculation that groundwork for the 2016 rallies had been laid during the previous eight years by the Tea Party. A national poll conducted in 2010 showed that 43 percent of white rural voters supported the Tea Party, compared with only 19 percent of white urban voters. Support in white suburbs (38 percent) was only slightly lower than among white rural voters, though, confirming ethnographic studies showing strong interest among retirees, semi-skilled workers, and persons experiencing job loss in those places.[2] Rallies were held in smaller towns, but the larger ones naturally occurred in larger places. In Texas, for example, the largest rally occurred at the Southfork Ranch near Dallas with an estimated fifty thousand in attendance. Other large rallies occurred in medium-sized cities such as Austin, Corpus Christi, Longview, and Wichita Falls.

Interviews in smaller towns showed two factors that contributed to mobilization there. One was networking and ease of travel, which enabled small-town residents to attend rallies in larger locations. The other was leadership, usually from preachers who organized their congregations. They were mostly pastors of white evangelical congregations. In national data, born-again Christians' odds of favoring the Tea Party were two and a half times greater than among other respondents, taking into consideration differences in race, gender, marital status, income, and age. Like other Tea Party supporters, they did not like Washington, did not like high taxes, and did not like Obama.[3] Besides that, they appealed to "biblical principles," drew on networks such as the American Family Association and Grassroots America previously established to promote pro-life issues and oppose same-sex marriage.[4] In Texas they favored Rick Perry for president in 2012 and Ted Cruz for the U.S. Senate. In other places they mobilized for conservative Republicans. They agreed that things in Washington were out of control. A few preached that Obama was the anti-Christ.

Most of the outrage we heard in our interviews, though, was the kind people talked about at the coffee shop or after church, rather than the kind that motivated them to join the "radicals" who participated in boisterous rallies. Perhaps they were glad to hear about a vocal group speaking up even if they were not part of that group. For the average person it was enough to affect how they voted, sometimes to switch party affiliations or to opt for a more conservative candidate than the incumbent in primary elections. They felt it strongly enough and personally enough that it was part of the local culture. They were collectively outraged both as residents of their own community and as members of rural America.

5

Moral Decline

In many of the rural towns I studied, the prevailing view was that morality in America is seriously declining. The decline was evident, people said, in dishonest dealings in Washington and on Wall Street. It was clear in the sexual promiscuity portrayed by Hollywood, the availability of pornography on the Internet, and the growing prevalence of crude language on television. They considered moral decline a threat to their communities even though they mostly saw it happening elsewhere. It violated their sense of how a good community should behave and worried them because of its corrosive effects.

Donna Graber is a hairstylist who works at a small salon on Main Street near the courthouse in Newborough. She's lived here all her life—"since God knows when," she says, and loves the valley and the surrounding hills. She knows the town's early history by heart and has served on enough community-wide committees that she knows what people do for a living and where they work. Like the other people we talked to in Newborough, she says the village is a good, safe place to raise children and grandchildren and she acknowledges that the community is content to not be growing, even though it is currently facing a bit of a financial crunch and has lost its grocery store and the quaint historic hotel that used to draw tourists. She personally would like to see some efforts to attract new people. It would help her business. But the town's demography is not her main concern.

Her main concern is the moral decline she sees spreading through the nation. She's not apocalyptic about it. She doesn't think it means the whole society is falling apart. It just seems to her that somehow the moral climate has changed over the past twenty or thirty years, whether you think about individuals or families or the government. People need to be completely honest and follow the law, she says. "I follow the Ten Commandments to the best I can. Those are just my personal beliefs. If you follow the Ten Commandments you are pretty good."

The trouble now, she says, is that people aren't teaching their children good morals and when they get out of the house the problems start. "You need to take care of the problems in your own house. It all starts in your own home."

But even if you want to train your children to have good morals, you can't, she thinks. The government steps in and tells you what you can and cannot do. "You can't spank your children. You can't discipline your own child the way you feel you should without them being able to call the county. And now the kid has the right over the parent. The parents should have the right to control their own home."

ALLIGATORS IN THE SWAMP

In various versions Mrs. Graber's concerns about moral decline surfaced again and again in our conversations with people around the country. "Everyone is just out for themselves. There isn't that basic human kindness and dignity we relied on in the past when times were hard. Your neighbor would usually be there for you, but that seems to be getting suppressed." This was the view of a woman in another New England town who holds an office position at the courthouse and whose husband works at a blue-collar job. "It's attacking the moral fiber of the country and those rips in the fabric are becoming almost too large to mend. It's very scary."

"You feel like your arms are getting pulled out of your sockets," another woman explained. "You're trying to do what you can to keep things together. You need to do something to turn things around and get people back on track." She didn't know what the answer was. "It's very unnerving."

Talk of moral decline sounds like a theme from politically conservative television programs. But by no means was it only a conservative theme among the people we interviewed. Consider Brent Miller. He went to college at the University of California, Berkeley, in the 1960s during the heyday of campus radicalism. He now lives in San Lopez, a small West Coast community that has attracted people seeking refuge from the cities and has always prided itself on its progressive views. Yet he is convinced there is severe moral decline in America. "I probably contributed to it, growing up in the 1960s and going to Berkeley," he muses. "I have to own some responsibility." He explains that he grew up having to go to church and he gives religion credit for trying to create a workable social order in which you put people together and keep them from acting like wild animals. It provided moral guidelines, but then he, like many others of his generation, abandoned religion. It was too rigid, too confining.

"I believe we have by and large substituted television for the church," he says. "Television gets far more undivided attention than the church ever hoped to get. And the moral lessons taught on television are at the root of the moral decline in this country." He thinks television does a good job of entertaining us but it provides nothing in the way of community responsibility that the church tried to offer or even of the neighborly social bonds he appreciates about his own community. "We're just losing faith in any kind of higher moral accountability."

The clergy we talked with would not have agreed with Mr. Miller that the church's moral guidelines were unworkable, but they did overwhelmingly agree about the nation's moral decline. Whether they were Protestants or Catholics or pastors of small, struggling congregations or large, flourishing churches, they expressed worries that went beyond the usual concerns about sinfulness and selfishness and pride. They saw signs of moral decay in the nation at large and in their own communities. And as community leaders, they felt it necessary to speak their minds about what was happening.

Reverend Lauren Davis offered a particularly articulate view of what was happening. She grew up on a dairy farm near Newborough and majored in animal science in college, but soon after graduating felt a call from God to devote her life to Christian ministry. She went to seminary and in addition to becoming a wife and mother took a position as the pastor of an independent church in one of the smaller villages not far from Newborough.

"It almost feels like the biblical prophecies are coming true in our nation," she says. "I hope that's not the case. But I've said over and over that the only hope I see for this country is a great awakening." She means a time of turning to God, like the Great Awakening that swept the American colonies in the 1730s and 1740s.

She feels terribly discouraged. "I sacrificed heavily to go into the ministry. I left the family farm that was in our family for generations. I left the thing I loved. I wanted to be part of that kind of great awakening, but I haven't seen much impact. I feel like I have my finger in the dike and I can't pull it out, but I can't stand here forever."

"Our culture continues to decline, our families continue to break apart, our schools continually do worse and worse. The churches are hurting. The economy is suffering. Politics are alarming. I haven't been able to drain the swamp. The alligators are everywhere."

Reverend Davis talks about these issues with her congregation. She tries to avoid communicating how despondent she feels, telling them instead how we need a spiritual awakening and that we are in trouble without it. She isn't sure what they hear, but she believes they are shocked and appalled and baffled by what's happening in the world around them and even in the community.

One of the people who agrees strongly with Reverend Davis is Lyle Eads, a farmer who serves on the village council in Newborough. He says he's not a highly religious person, but it bothers him that religion in the whole country seems to be systematically pushed to the back burner. "This country was founded on Christian principles," he asserts. "The blueprint for treating people right was based on Christian principles. But now you have all these laws and regulations. You can't do this and you can't do that. We've taken the fear of God out of everything."

The laws and regulations Mr. Eads is referring to mostly concern separation of church and state. In interview after interview people talked about how bad it was that prayer had been pushed out of the public schools and the Ten Commandments could no longer be taught. This was their clearest complaint about how the government was contributing to the nation's moral decline.

In the town of Oakley, a community of ten thousand surrounded by treeless fields, oil wells, and an abandoned air base, John Franklin lamented the laissez-faire attitude about God and God's expectations of individuals he saw contributing to the moral decline of America. Unlike some of the people we talked with who thought faith and morality were private matters between the individual and God, Mr. Franklin felt strongly that God needed to be honored in the "public arena" for religion to have an impact on public morality. By public, he meant including prayer and Bible reading and teaching the Ten Commandments in public schools and opening community events with prayer. "At our local high school games we still have prayer before a game," he said, "and we try to get students involved in planning their own school services and having student-led prayer at the flagpole in the morning." But he said the community felt stymied because decisions about these things were no longer at the local level. The frustration was with the "legal parameters that the federal government has handed down."

There is a notion that concern about moral decline is a feature of small-town life because the people there see their communities on the skids and would like things to return to a time when everything was better. That notion may bear some truth, but it is hardly the whole story. Many of the communities where people lamented the decay of morality were doing just fine demographically and economically. And they were by no means the only ones with that view. Perhaps it was only their disappointment in the politics of 2016, but urban progressives seemed given to the belief that things were not going well either.

The connection with rural America's outrage at Washington is that it would be nice to think that in the face of moral decline, Washington was doing something about it instead of aggravating the problem. The soberest minds who offered their opinions on the topic knew the decline would not be staunched by the triumph of one political party or the other. They knew the challenge of turning things around had to start in families and schools and communities. They just hoped Washington wouldn't stand in the way—or make things worse.

Reverend Jane Ewing, a pastor in one of the farming villages near Fairfield, put it best: "We've become a society of fear and anger rather than a nation of let's get along and do things together for the good of the country," she said. "It's not helpful. It's not enabling us to live as we should in community."

ABORTION

When rural Americans talk specifically about the kinds of moral decline that bothers them, abortion is at the top of their list. Of course, they are not alone in this. Many of the large rallies against abortion have taken place in cities and suburbs, and the main battles in recent years have been fought in state legislatures. Nevertheless, sentiment against abortion runs particularly high in small towns. Indeed, evidence from national surveys shows that the odds of being against abortion under all circumstances with only the exception of rape or incest rises steadily as town size decreases, taking into account other differences due to age, gender, education, and region. Compared to cities of at least 250,000, the odds of opposing abortion in the smallest towns are more than three times higher.[1]

In 2009 when abortion provider Dr. George Tiller was shot and killed in suburban Wichita at the Reformation Lutheran Church where he was a member, I was conducting research for *Red State Religion*, a book about conservative religion and politics in Kansas. The tragic killing provided an occasion to interview people before and after the murder on their views about abortion. Not surprisingly, most abhorred the killing, but held strong views about abortion that they were eager to express. More opposed abortion than voiced support for a woman's right to choose. In retrospect, though, the murder marked a turning point not only in Kansas but across the nation in a fast-paced effort to shift the terms in how abortion is discussed.[2]

The murder in many ways represented the culmination of more than two decades of anti-abortion activism in Wichita, the most notable of which was the so-called Summer of Mercy organized by Operation Rescue in 1991 during which more than three thousand activists were arrested. When Operation Rescue left, the activism continued, organized largely by several large Protestant and Catholic churches. In 1993 Tiller was shot and wounded but returned to work the next day. Televangelists Jerry Falwell and Pat Robertson made visits to Wichita to lend support and to argue that abortion would be rolled back despite its support in Washington.

As the Religious Right's opposition to abortion continued to mobilize, it gained strength from additional statewide and national "pro-life" organizations. In the 1998 Kansas gubernatorial election, 79 percent of those polled said moral decay in their communities was serious and 72 percent said they were interested in candidates' positions on moral values. Both candidates declared their opposition to abortion.

A decade later it had become nearly a foregone conclusion in Kansas and in many other predominantly Republican states that no Republican candidate could win without opposing abortion and that doing so was a proven way to achieve victory even when other issues such as economic policies might also be of concern. It was this ability of so-called values voters to swing elections that prompted Thomas Frank in 2004 to answer that "what's the matter with Kansas" was the prevalence of right-wing ideological activists in the churches and in local government.

Interviews in rural Kansas and in small towns in other states in 2009 revealed that the struggle over abortion had evolved to the point that four main positions could be identified. The first was composed of activists who played leadership roles in their communities and forged links among small communities and with supporters in cities and suburbs. Many of the activists in small towns were local clergy whose leadership in congregations gave them a built-in audience. They held prayer vigils and lobbied legislators in state capitals and showed their disdain for the U.S. Supreme Court by organizing large marches in Washington each January. They also preached against abortion to their congregations, held local vigils, and found ways to declare the sinfulness of abortion with vivid examples.

A Catholic priest in Newborough, for example, said it was well-known in the community that a church-going woman a few years ago had an abortion. He wasn't sympathetic. He said he would never refer to her by name in speaking to his congregation, but he didn't have to. The abortion was merely a symptom of everything else that good people should deplore. The woman was divorced, sexually promiscuous, and slept around until eventually she got pregnant and then decided to terminate the pregnancy. It was appalling that someone who had seemed to embrace a conservative value system would do this. "She cast off all restraint and behaved in a way that's just wholly contradictory to everything she professed to believe."

He of course was celibate, but his views were shared by many of the men, clergy and non-clergy alike, who were married. Abortion in their view was murder. It was killing a baby. They could see no circumstances at all under which it could be justified, not even rape or incest or to save the life of the mother. Implicitly, women who sought abortions were weak, immoral, deficient in performing their responsibilities as mothers. And doctors who helped them should be put out of business—or worse. As one of the Southern Baptist anti-abortion activists put it, "George Tiller was a calloused murderer. He personally murdered eighty thousand babies." He wishes politicians would define abortion as murder. That way Tiller could have been tried and executed legally.

The second group included the ordinary residents who firmly opposed abortion. They generally summarized their views succinctly, almost as if they had declared themselves against abortion so many times that they were weary of discussing the topic despite feeling strongly about it. They summarized their position with phrases such as "life is sacred," "life is precious," "life begins at conception," "I'm pro-life," "I believe it's a baby," and "I don't believe in killing." For them the issue was cut and dried, usually settled in scripture or by the church, just as obeying the Ten Commandments and wives being obedient to their husbands was. Many felt abortion simply didn't make sense, either, because, as a homemaker in Fairfield put it, "A lot of people want children and can't have them." Said another, "Promote adoption. Support pregnancy crisis centers." She'd participated in Wichita's "Summer of Mercy" when she was younger. But now she was glad the pro-life movement was shifting gears and doing more to encourage adoption.

Most of the residents who strongly opposed abortion said their position would influence how they voted, even though they were not personally engaged in pro-life activism, and they felt that most of the people in their community felt the same way they did. Usually the vocal support for their opposition came at church. Abortion was something they needed to talk about, most of the clergy said. And it could be talked about in church without the conversation ever having to be explicitly political. As a pastor in Texas explained, "I preach about abortion as a theological issue. I don't have to turn around then and say vote Republican."

The third group was pro-choice. They were diverse, ranging from those who thought abortion was a bad choice but sometimes not the worst option to others who said they would never personally have an abortion but didn't believe in judging others. They sometimes knew a woman who had an abortion and respected her for having made a terribly difficult decision. This group differed from the pro-life group in offering more complicated thoughts on the matter that reflected mixed feelings and uncertainty and that also suggested having had to come up with opinions without much local support. For that reason, they acknowledged also being reluctant to express their opinions locally.

The fourth group fell into the category of a-plague-on-both-your-houses. Some were privately pro-life and some were privately pro-choice. But they were tired of the issue. It was the elephant in the room that just kept dominating discussions at church and in politics. They not only wanted it to be resolved, to go away somehow, but were also disdainful of people who took strong vocal stands on it one way or the other.

Karen Meeks, the farm woman near Fairfield, stated it best. "When you have an unwanted pregnancy, none of your options is good, but it's become a very emotional hot-button issue for some people. That's because it doesn't affect them personally, so they can think of it as a big deal. Because you don't do it, you feel better about yourself. If someone else does it, they're a terrible person and you feel better about yourself."

Why people fit one or another of these categories had more to do with their religion than anything else. Church was about the only place abortion was discussed openly and repeatedly. Pro-life people didn't discuss it much elsewhere because they assumed nearly everyone in their community agreed with them. Pro-choice people didn't because they assumed nearly everyone disagreed. And the plague-on-it people didn't because they wanted the issue to go away.

Religion mattered because except in the smallest towns there was enough religious diversity that people heard one view at one church and people who went to a different church might hear a different view. Fairfield, with several dozen churches in town and a dozen more in surrounding villages, was the best example of this diversity. Several of the Catholics we spoke with, for example, were adamantly pro-life and when asked why, their first response was simply "I'm Catholic." A member of an evangelical Protestant church said she was pro-life because "God put it in me" what is right and wrong. It was such an obvious position for her that she couldn't understand anyone thinking differently. "You have people in California who say it's wrong to declaw cats and have a law against it, and they're probably the same people who think it's just fine to suck a baby's brains out. I just don't understand people like that!"

The abortion opponents who offered more than succinct summary phrases went beyond the argument about abortion being murder to suggest an additional aspect of the problem that related to their views about small-town people needing to take responsibility for themselves. Richard Pruitt, the man who runs a jobs training program in Fairfield, provided the clearest example. He is a Roman Catholic who adamantly believes that abortion is always wrong. He says his views reflect those of the church and are summarized simply in the phrase "respect for life." Yet when pressed to unpack his beliefs an important assumption surfaced. The woman who gets pregnant is in his estimation not behaving responsibly, first, toward herself, and second, toward the baby, who deserves to live and should be placed with an adoptive family. That sense of irresponsibility, he says, makes him angry. The reason is not what a specific woman or doctor does. It is rather what abortion symbolizes. "Morals just seem to be going downhill. That bothers me. It really does."

Quite different views were expressed by people affiliated with mainline Christian, Episcopal, Presbyterian, Lutheran, and Mennonite churches. A member of the Christian church, for instance, who had had a stillborn baby and received support from her church, felt because of the complex circumstances under which an abortion might make sense that she was more pro-choice than pro-life. Similarly, a Mennonite said he doesn't like to see the situations that give rise to abortion, but has been close enough to such situations to recognize how complicated the decision is.

Nobody felt abortion was not a moral issue. Whether they were pro-life or pro-choice, they considered abortion an important moral problem. It had been discussed so often by activists and in churches that they knew what side they were on. The ones who truly blamed the Supreme Court for allowing abortions were angry that more hadn't been done to stop them. On both sides, it was clear that they felt the politics of the issue were out of their hands.

HOMOSEXUALITY

Homosexuality is the other topic that many rural Americans consider a vexing moral concern. Data from a national survey show that support for a constitutional amendment banning gay marriage rises steadily as the size of communities in which people live decreases, taking account of other differences in gender, race, education, age, and region. The odds of supporting an anti-gay marriage amendment are more than twice as high in rural communities of fewer than a thousand people as they are in cities of 250,000 people or more. Many of the states in which state-level constitutional bans on same-sex marriage were passed—Alabama, Arkansas, Kansas,

Kentucky, Nebraska, North Dakota, and Oklahoma—have large rural populations.[3]

Like opposition to abortion, negative attitudes toward homosexuality and opposition to marriage equality is for many rural Americans rooted in conservative religious beliefs. Typical responses to the question why they opposed homosexuality included "church," "the Bible says it's wrong," "my Christian background," and "God is not pleased with it."

Believing that homosexuality was unbiblical gave people reason enough to be against it in the abstract. They could vote for political candidates who agreed with them on general principles, feeling they were helping in a small way to impede the nation's moral decline. When it became a threat to their community, they usually added the argument that homosexuality was undermining family values, perhaps even more so than abortion. The family, after all, was basic not only to morality in general but also to the well-being of their community. Homosexuality threatened the traditional family in much the same way as divorce, sexual promiscuity, abortion, and teenage rebellion. It was a subversive idea—a kind of permissive "anything goes" thinking—that made it harder for parents to teach their children what was right.

"It's just pretty sick," one of the blue-collar workers we spoke with declared, adding, "We try to teach our kids that it's wrong, because my boy has asked about it. He's seven and he asked about it because it's on TV all the time. He asked why two guys are kissing and we have to explain to him that marriage is between a man and a woman; it's not proper with anyone else."

An important difference from abortion, though, is the fact that many people in rural communities know someone who is gay, whereas they rarely knew someone personally who had an abortion. In fact, a national survey in 2006 found that in rural counties 88 percent said they knew someone who was gay, and among that 88 percent, 20 percent said the person they knew was a family member, 22 percent said the person was a close friend, 14 percent said the person was a co-worker, and 4 percent said they themselves were gay.[4]

Research on prejudice toward people unlike yourself shows that knowing someone personally usually has a significant effect in reducing prejudice. That was evident in numerous cases among the people we interviewed. Reverend Patterson in Gulfdale is one such case. In his preaching, he naturally emphasizes the Word of God, which he feels strongly about, including what it says about sin. The moral decline he sees all around in the culture, especially the view that we should be more open to lifestyles that are not biblical, concerns him deeply. And that pertains particularly to homosexuality, which he regards as sin. "I have always been a strong advocate about what the Bible says about homosexuality," he asserts.

But Reverend Patterson's brother-in-law is gay and is now in a nursing home. "A few weeks ago when I visited my brother-in-law, his partner looked at me and said he appreciated me treating him like a fellow human being, even though he knew that we saw homosexuality differently. I shared that with my congregation. I said, 'That was a sense of what Jesus would have done.' I saw the compassion from my brother-in-law's partner from me respecting him." The encounter didn't change Reverend Patterson's belief that homosexuality is sin; in his own telling, it was something he was still thinking about, but it had at least prompted a bit of reflection.

The reflection that went a step further toward acceptance stemmed from considering whether homosexuality was biologically determined, in addition to knowing people who were gay. A homemaker in Fairfield who attended a Catholic church and sent her children to a Catholic school gave one of the best responses when asked what had shaped her views about homosexuality. She listed three influences: knowing people who were gay, her church's teachings about not being judgmental, and thinking that homosexuality was probably not a choice. "I can't understand why some people feel so strongly about it," she said. "I can't feel that it could be completely wrong because I've known lots of people who were gay and I don't understand why they would be made that way if it was really wrong. Maybe it's something wired." She concluded, "I don't feel that I should condemn them; they're people!"

If knowing someone who was gay didn't prompt a more accepting attitude, it did sometimes encourage heterosexual people to reframe the issue enough to lower the vehemence with which they opposed homosexuality. The evangelical Protestant woman in Fairfield who described abortion as sucking babies' brains out, for instance, offered a surprisingly milder opinion about homosexuality. "I think homosexuality is a sin," she said, "but I think there are a lot of other things that are sin, too. God expects us to try to not be sinful, but I know we are sinful no matter what." She added, "And just for the record, I have homosexuals in my family."

Holding moderately tolerant views in private is one thing, but that fails to take account of the strong pressure that small-town norms can impose on gay people in these communities as well as on people who might in other circumstances be more accepting. For instance, one of the people we interviewed, who was gay, had grown up in a small town and was glad to leave as quickly as he could. In high school, he was the only boy who didn't play football. Sitting on the sidelines, he knew everybody thought he was "different." He still finds it nearly impossible to visit his home community without feeling shunned.

Without saying so explicitly, his experience reflected what studies suggest about a kind of macho culture prevailing in rural communities. Being gay is difficult not only because football is the way to be a small-town hero but also because boys are expected to participate in other sports and exude masculinity in how they talk about themselves. One of the farmers we spoke with said it had been a real adjustment having a gay son, not only because his son was gay, but also because his son did not want to farm.

A farmer in another small town said he had gotten to know many people who were gay while serving in the Navy and working in a city for five years before returning to his home community. "I've known people who are gay and are nice people and I've known other people who were gay and they weren't such nice people," he said. "I really think it's genetics. I figure live and let live."

He had a hired man a few years ago who was gay, though, and he fired him. "It wasn't because he wasn't doing a good job and it wasn't because he was gay. I was afraid of what might happen in the community. What if he molested a young boy! I'd feel responsible because I was the one who brought him into the community!"

Well before the U.S. Supreme Court decision in 2015 guaranteeing a right to same-sex marriage, it was evident that attitudes were gradually shifting in some of the rural communities I studied. As the topic was discussed in religious denominations and in state and national elections, people in rural communities said two things had happened. One was that opponents dug in their heels. They were angry that President Obama, military leaders, and others in Washington were expressing greater support for the rights of homosexuals. It was particularly distressing to them to think about homosexuals gaining power as an organized political movement.

The other effect, though, was that people in rural communities began to see that there were differences of opinion even in their own communities and their own churches, and those differences prompted some new thinking. Mr. Somers in Newborough, for instance, was convinced that this had been the main effect in his community. Until ten or fifteen years ago, he said, nobody in Newborough said much of anything about homosexuality. It just wasn't a front burner issue. "Now, though, it is an issue because it ought to be; we're talking about it. And slowly, there's no question that the views are moderating."

The principal reason it was being talked about in Newborough was the debate taking place in churches. At the denominational level, Methodists, Episcopalians, Lutherans, and Presbyterians were all spending time at their national meetings discussing gay ordination for clergy, same-sex marriage, and related issues. The denominations mandated that local congregations discuss the issues as well. That meant people who quietly supported one side or the other had to make their positions known. Several of the congregations in and around Newborough split as a result. Members who strongly opposed homosexuality left and joined more conservative congregations or started new ones. But members who stayed found reasons to stay despite their disagreements.

Reverend C. C. Willis's Lutheran congregation went through the process and came out better for it even though it was difficult and several of the members left. As the denomination discussed the issues and took various votes, the congregation decided that getting along as a congregation and as residents of a small community was more important than taking strong positions on one side or the other. It didn't advertise itself as a "welcoming" congregation, which disappointed some of its members, and it didn't take a stand against homosexuality, which disappointed others. Instead, it tried to focus on relating to people with greater acceptance whoever they were.

"When I listen to some people and some pastors who take a single issue and treat it like a life or death issue," Reverend Willis says, "I say, 'you've got to be kidding me.' What most concerns me every day is dealing with people. No matter what the issue is, how it affects the person is a heck of a lot more important than 'the issue.'"

As discussions like this took place in rural communities, people with long-held views about homosexuality sometimes found themselves thinking about the topic in new ways. One of the more vivid examples was a woman in her seventies in Fairfield who had never heard anyone in her community being accepting toward homosexuals. Yet, she said she'd been hearing more about it and learning about it lately, which was causing her to think differently about same-sex marriage. "If you're committed to an individual who is giving you the opportunity to be their support system in ways legally that you couldn't otherwise," she said, "I can see how helpful that would be for committed people."

There was a paradox in all this, though. On the one hand, the conversations about gay rights and marriage equality wouldn't have happened in rural communities, people admitted, if there hadn't been prompting from the outside—from church boards, political discussions, constitutional referenda, and the like. Absent those external influences, the local culture in rural communities would have taken it for granted that nearly everyone was on the same page in simply considering homosexuality a sin. On the other hand, it was precisely these outside promptings that rural communities disliked, just as they did Washington telling them to purchase healthcare and quit reading the Ten Commandments in school. They found those intrusions on their local autonomy distasteful, not only because they may have disagreed with them but also because they violated local norms of working things out with local circumstances in mind.

Reverend Willis was perhaps more upset about these outside influences than most, having experienced them from his denomination as well as from government. His conviction that he was stubbornly going to do what he thought was right for the people in his own congregation provided the counterpoint for what he thought about Washington. "Who the heck knows who's telling the truth and what's going on behind the scenes," he said about hot-button issues such as same-sex marriage being debated in the nation's capital. Those social issues are always going to be political, and if you want to go down that road, you're going to have an argument. To me, what matters is dealing with people, not the quote-unquote 'issues.'"

AGAINST SELF-INTEREST?

The important question Thomas Frank raised in *What's the Matter with Kansas?* is whether people in the rural heartland—especially ones without college degrees—have been so obsessed with abortion and homosexuality that they voted against their economic self-interest. Would they have been better off, for instance, to have voted for candidates who voted down right-to-work laws and supported unions, better schools, and a welfare safety net for the poor?

Hypotheticals of that kind are interesting to speculate about but hard to prove or disprove. Kansans did have a Democratic governor in Kathleen Sibelius at the time Frank's book was published and during her six years in office she supported much of the agenda Frank had in mind. His critique was best directed at the conservative state legislature. On the national scene, Frank's argument fit best with Karl Rove's successful strategy in the 2004 presidential campaign to secure reelection for George W. Bush by promoting anti-gay referenda that increased the turnout among evangelicals and other conservative Republicans. The best statistical test of Frank's thesis gave it only limited support in the South; otherwise, there was no evidence that "values" issues such as abortion and homosexuality outweighed economic issues.[5]

None of that bears as directly on rural voters as it does on blue-collar voters in cities—the kind Frank thought would have been better off as he toured the empty parking lots of abandoned aircraft factories in Wichita. The rural voters in my interviews occasionally said they would vote for candidates who did not oppose abortion and homosexuality, but those comments were rare. In most cases, they said they would only vote for pro-life, anti-gay candidates. And if they did, the fact that small communities nationally were decidedly more likely than large cities to oppose abortion and favor a constitutional ban on same-sex marriage suggests that rural voters did contribute to conservative Republican victories. Indeed, the gap between small towns voting for Republican presidential candidates and large cities and suburbs voting for Democratic candidates was widening ever since Reagan had appealed to voters across the board in the 1980s.

For rural voters, though, it is hard to make a credible claim that by voting based on issues such as abortion and homosexuality they were voting against their self-interest. Although many rural communities have small manufacturing plants, hardly any of these are unionized. Jobs training programs would likely have had limited success in small towns. And Republican farm policies were generally more appealing to farmers and townspeople dependent on farms anyway than Democratic policies.

Adjudicating how rural voters should have voted only in terms of economic self-interest, though, runs counter to the larger argument I have been making about the importance of moral cultures in rural communities. The cultural compact that holds rural communities together consists in important measure in agreement about basic moral principles, such as honesty, hard work, neighborliness, and faith, as well as tacit agreement on social norms such as being friendly and participating in community events. Our interviews in small towns showed that nearly everyone felt that the prevailing norm in their community included opposing abortion—so much so that people with pro-choice views kept their opinions to themselves. Until recently, the implicit norm about homosexuality also held that it should be opposed. These were among the agreements that townspeople believed they shared and believed were not shared by many Americans elsewhere, especially in cities and in Washington.

The most explicit support for these agreements about abortion and homosexuality, as well as for the belief that morality in the wider world is declining, is religion, particularly participation in conservative Catholic parishes and evangelical Protestant congregations. This grounding, as I've suggested, was evident in the interviews with laypeople and clergy in rural communities. It is well established in numerous national polls and surveys, too. Indeed, much of the mobilization for pro-life and anti-gay voting has occurred through state, regional, and national organizations with close ties to local churches.[6]

The question of self-interest in rural communities must be considered, therefore, in relation to religion and not just to such hot-button issues as abortion and homosexuality. In opposing abortion and homosexuality most church members in rural communities are also agreeing with what they hear in congregations. Religion is part of the moral warp and woof of where they live, which means that supporting it is understandably in their self-interest. Religion plays an important role in holding the community together, whether in preaching and potlucks or conducting weddings and funerals. It supports the family values that people hold dear and tells them that they should care for their neighbors.

It is in the caring for neighbors, though, that a difficulty arises. None of the clergy we interviewed said it was wrong to care for the poor and needy. Nearly all their churches had programs to assist indigent members and a few others in the community who might need help from time to time. Many of the congregations, including some of the smallest ones in the smallest towns, supported an occasional foreign missionary and occasionally sent a youth member on a short-term overseas mission trip. That was all consistent with the churches' teachings about caring for the needy.

What the clergy and lay members usually missed seeing was that how they voted also affected provisions for the
needy. The conservative Republicans they voted for because
of acceptable positions on abortion and homosexuality also
were the ones in many instances that opposed welfare spending, favored regressive tax policies, and gerrymandered dis-
tricts to limit the political influence of African Americans and
Hispanics.

That was a blind spot in cities as well as in rural communities. It was consistent with the view that Washington means
big government and that big government is bad. It was consistent with the small-town view that local charity and volunteering were better than government programs. In predominantly white rural communities it was easier to think locally
than to recognize how closely linked local voting was to state
and national policies.

6

Bigotry

On October 14, 2016, the FBI arrested three right-wing militants who were plotting to bomb an apartment building in Garden City, Kansas, killing dozens of immigrant Somali meatpacking plant workers and hoping to initiate a bloodbath against immigrants across the nation.

Five years earlier I had conducted research in Garden City and written a detailed history of the community in *Remaking the Heartland*. At about the same time several other social scientists also did studies in Garden City. Despite its remote location in southwest Kansas, the community was a magnet for researchers interested in immigration. Since 1980, the largest meat-processing facility in the world was located there and half the community's population were recent immigrants. Before that, Garden City had been of interest for a different reason. In 1959, four members of the Herbert Clutter family who lived on a farm a few miles from Garden City were brutally murdered. Truman Capote's *In Cold Blood* memorialized the event.

I was as shocked as anyone at the news of the bombing plot in 2016. My research had unearthed several reports of secretive militias in western Kansas. But Garden City was one of the success stories in rural America's adaptation to large numbers of new immigrants. In 1980 when the meat-processing plant opened, only 14 percent of Garden City's population was Hispanic. During the plant's first three years of operation nearly twenty-five hundred new residents arrived, nearly all Hispanic. By 1990, 25 percent of the population was Hispanic and by the end of the century that number swelled to 43 percent. The town's rapid population growth strained the school system and created a severe housing shortage. Long-term residents grumbled about the changes. And yet, the transition was exceptionally smooth.

The 2016 presidential campaign raised but left unanswered the question of whether anger was festering among people who feel left out and left behind to the point that bigotry against immigrants, Muslims, African Americans, and even women played a role in the election. The best evidence suggests that it did not, at least not on a large scale, but there seemed to be plenty of people who, given the chance, were eager to seize the opportunity to proclaim their concern that "whiteness" was under attack.[1]

Garden City's experience suggests the necessity of looking closely at how rural America is adapting to greater ethnic, racial, and religious diversity and whether rural communities that have been predominantly white are experiencing these changes as threats. On the one hand, the community's success holds lessons about why adaptation has been easier in some rural communities than others. On the other hand, the fact that a bombing plot could be hatched in the same community necessitates asking pointed questions about the role of inflamed political rhetoric in emboldening bigotry and violence.

IMMIGRATION

The image of rural America being overwhelmingly white Anglo and thus an obvious location for bigotry to flourish is true at least as far as the demographic makeup is concerned. In 1980, white Anglos made up 91.3 percent of the population nationally of all small rural communities with total populations under twenty-five thousand. By 2010, the white Anglo proportion had declined only to 86.5 percent. Over this thirty-year period, the African American proportion remained constant at only 6 percent. The Hispanic proportion, however, more than doubled during this period, from 2.5 percent to 6.1 percent. Much of this increase occurred in small towns in Texas, New Mexico, Arizona, and California, but proportionally large increases also occurred in Minnesota and North Carolina.

By 2010, Hispanics averaged 20 percent of the total in larger rural communities like Garden City with populations of at least ten thousand. In 1980, only 454 rural communities were at least 20 percent Hispanic, but by 2010 this number had more than doubled, to 1,102. Among all rural towns, 40 percent in 2010 included at least a few immigrants from Latin America. In all rural communities, the average number who had been born in Mexico was 175.[2]

The principal reason for large concentrations of Hispanic immigrants in rural communities like Garden City is the growth of the meat and poultry processing industry. Instead of shipping live cattle to Kansas City and Chicago for slaughter, and instead of raising poultry on small farms, large companies—IBP (Iowa Beef Processors), National Beef, and Tyson, among others—built huge processing plants in right-to-work states like Arkansas, Kansas, and South Dakota, hiring immigrant workers at dirt-cheap wages. By 2006, nearly a hundred plants each employing more than five hundred workers were scattered across these and adjacent states. Most were in towns the size of Garden City or smaller, which meant that an influx of low-wage immigrant workers had a profound impact on community dynamics.

Besides the processed food industry relocating to small towns, rural America is also profoundly indebted to immigrant laborers working at low-wage jobs in towns, at construction sites, and on farms. Our interviews encountered community after community that was heavily dependent on immigrants, whether to tend orchards, to work in feedlots, to clean milking machines, or to staff filling stations.

The response of white Anglo populations in rural communities to the growing number of Hispanic immigrants was evident in a national survey conducted in 2003. Among the approximately three thousand randomly selected nationally representative adults in the survey, nearly five hundred were white Anglos living in rural counties.[3]

On the one hand, 66 percent of rural respondents said they would welcome Hispanics becoming a stronger presence in the United States in the next few years, only slightly fewer than the 74 percent who said this in metropolitan areas. This response was consistent with many of the comments people offered in interviews. For example, Mr. Somers in Newborough grew up working with Hispanics on his dad's farm and most of his employees currently are Hispanics, many of whom are recent immigrants. His experience has been nothing but positive.

"These are people who left intolerable situations at home where they had high unemployment and no opportunities;

they came to a foreign country to work as hard as they could as many hours as they could to earn a living to feed their families," he says. "By and large, they deserve a medal." He considers it deplorable that more isn't done to help them come legally, which leads him to be understanding of the ones who are undocumented.

"You could build a ten-foot-high fence across the border with Mexico," he says, which wouldn't work "because if there's a way someone can go find a job opportunity to feed his family, he's going to do it. Our country's reluctance to face the facts is why we have the problems we do. Nobody in Washington seems willing to face the real story here."

Perhaps it was easy for Mr. Somers to be sympathetic since his farm benefited from immigrant labor. However, many of the farmers who didn't hire immigrants felt the same way. For instance, Glenn Evans, a Midwestern wheat farmer, shared Mr. Somers's opinion and raised it one. "What the heck," he said, "you've got all these little towns that hold onto their Swedish heritage or their German roots and now they don't like Mexicans because they're from Mexico and want to hang onto *their* heritage? Give me a break!"

"We've got these angry white people now. They're angry because we're losing control," he added. "Yes, I'm a vanishing breed, a white American male. I'm going to be in the minority. But thank goodness! These people are bringing in new ideas, new energy. I'm glad America is still drawing new people!"

On the other hand, the national survey demonstrated that if the issue was cast as "immigrants" rather than "Hispanics," responses were quite different. Among white Anglos in rural communities, 70 percent favored passing a law to reduce the number of immigrants coming into the country (as did 65 percent of metropolitan respondents).

In communities like Garden City with large numbers of immigrants, the responses ranged widely. In one community of nine thousand, nearly all of whom were white Anglo, half the population decamped within five years of a huge meat-processing plant bringing in large numbers of immigrants. In contrast, a town of twenty-five thousand was large enough that few of the white Anglo population left when the community became a meat-processing headquarters, but a citizens group formed to provide sanctuary for undocumented workers and an opposing group formed to track them down and deport them.

We found that clergy whose parishes include both immigrants and non-immigrants are among the most perceptive observers of relationships between the two. Father James Donahue, whose parish is in a town of eight thousand in which more than a third are Hispanic, is one of the clergy we met who was particularly candid about the divisiveness in his community. The way he saw it, problems stemmed from "old wounds and hurts and scars." He didn't say specifically what those were, but he thought there was a kind of general anger and fear about how the community was changing, for which immigrants and undocumented workers became easy targets. "People feel frustrated, helpless, and angry," he said, "and so the undocumented workers get blamed for everything—crime, drugs, no matter what, it's the immigrants."

Father Donahue had no doubt that white Anglos in his town were angry not only at Hispanic immigrants but also at the government. He says the church tries to help the immigrants who need food and housing, but they often need help in the form of public welfare. The white Anglos then complain, "Okay, you're Hispanic and we're Caucasian and you're getting all this help from government programs and nothing is happening for us and our kids."

The reasons Garden City's transition went as smoothly as it did was that the community drew on its tradition of being more inclusive than most and used that tradition to its advantage. Mexicans and African Americans had helped build the railroad that came through in the 1870s and by 1910, more than a hundred permanent residents from Mexico had settled to work in the sugar beet fields and sugar factory. By 1980, when the meat-processing plant opened, the county's population already included more than 3,400 Hispanics. There were also 7,000 Vietnamese immigrants.

Although Garden City experienced ethnic tensions in the 1980s and 1990s, the community expanded English-as-a-second-language programs in the schools, and the churches initiated Spanish language services and programs to help immigrants navigate the citizenship process. The most contested aspect of the community's transition was the meat plant's treatment of workers. Human Rights Watch investigations documented numerous violations. From the standpoint of ethnic relations, though, Garden City demonstrated the possibilities of diversity as being beneficial.

In 2011, A. G. Sulzberger of the *New York Times* visited communities near Garden City to see how they were adapting. "At first every community was very unwelcoming," one of the mayors told him, "but a lot of that was because we wanted to hold on so tight to what we were. In the last five years, we've seen that [Hispanic immigrants] are here, they're staying, they're part of the community. We've kind of gotten used to each other."[4]

Favorable sentiments such as this were by no means the only response. Some of the white Anglos we talked with in one of the nearby communities said they would not live in Garden City because of stories there about drugs, gangs, and violence. Garden City's mayor, a third-generation Mexican American, said there was still a lot of prejudice in the community. "People don't come out and say, 'I don't like Hispanics' or 'I don't like blacks,' but they find some other way to communicate it." He was sure some of it was ginned up by politics. When he ran for mayor, his opponent claimed he was an "illegal alien."

Whether they were immigrants or native-born residents, many of the Hispanics we spoke with made it clear that discrimination and the fear of friends and family being harassed or deported were of greater concern than bigoted remarks from white Anglos. They were well aware of families being torn apart and of raids in the middle of the night.

A Hispanic citizen we spoke with in Arizona described from personal experience what people living elsewhere knew about from headlines. His friend was twenty-six but had come to the United States illegally with his parents when he was two years old. "What law does a two-year-old break anyway?" He was the kind of person the sheriff liked to stop for a broken tail light and demand proof of citizenship.

Besides that, the slurs were nothing compared to the sacrifices people who otherwise were discriminated against made for their country. It was not just that fast food chains were benefiting from the harsh working conditions at slaughterhouses or that organic vegetables depended on stoop labor.

It was that family members were suffering and dying for their country.

Manuel Hernandez, the mayor of a town in Texas that was 70 percent Hispanic, put a fine point on it. "I have a child who has gone four times to Afghanistan," he said. "My son is fixing to go back for a fifth time. Last time I was in Washington, I asked my congressman, 'How many more times is my child going to have to go off and fight this war?' He couldn't answer."

MUSLIMS

Rural Americans' response to Muslims has been different from the response to Hispanic immigrants insofar as relatively few Muslims have settled in rural areas. In the national survey, the difference was evident in the fact that 53 percent of white Anglos claimed to have had a "great deal" or "fair amount" of personal contact with Latino Americans, whereas the comparable proportion having had personal contact with Muslims was only 15 percent. Attitudes toward Muslims were also conditioned by 9/11. Nearly half the respondents in both rural and metropolitan areas thought Muslims were "fanatical" and more than a third thought Muslims were "violent."

Surprisingly, since the survey was conducted only two years after 9/11, approximately half of rural and metropolitan respondents alike said they would welcome Muslims becoming a stronger presence in the United States. And, given the fact that Christianity is as strong as it is in rural America, it was also surprising that only a quarter of respondents in rural and metropolitan areas thought the influx of Muslims

and other non-Christians such as Hindus and Buddhists
would weaken Christianity, while a majority thought it would
strengthen Christianity.

How seemingly tolerant views like this could shift to the
point that calls for surveillance of Muslims, a ban on Muslim immigration, and possible prohibition on Muslim worship in the United States would become popular during the
2016 presidential election can be understood by probing
more deeply. Muslims as well as Hindus, Sikhs, and Buddhists interviewed at the time of the survey documented having been victims of hate crimes. Imams had been harassed
and mosques had been desecrated with graffiti and bombed.
A subsequent study of immigrants from Muslim and other
religious backgrounds who had become successful as lawyers,
doctors, educators, and business leaders showed that most
of them had also experienced prejudice and discrimination.[5]

The same research also suggested that Christian congregations that claimed to be interested in building bridges with
Muslims and other religious traditions were not doing so.
Churches located on the same block and sometimes sharing
a parking lot with a mosque or Hindu temple or Buddhist
meditation center had rarely made contact. The response was
like people in an elevator pressed together but denying one
another's presence. That was true of individuals, too, who figured some of their co-workers were probably Muslim but said
they never talked about religion.

In the absence of proactive steps by pluralistic Christian
groups to facilitate greater understanding and respect for
Muslims, the alternative was taken up by fundamentalists
and evangelical groups that regarded Muslims as danger-
ous followers of a false prophet. Indeed, one of the strongest

predictors of anti-Muslim and broader anti-immigrant attitudes in the survey was holding firmly to the conviction that only Christianity is true.

The other source of rising anti-Muslim sentiment was of course the successive outbreak of terrorist plots and the continuing wars in the Middle East, including the thousands of displaced persons seeking refuge and asylum. In rural America it was hardly the case that communities felt it likely that terrorism would occur locally. It was rather that concerns about Muslims connected with more generalized fears about threats to the American way of life that people hoped still prevailed in small towns and to convictions that leaders in Washington didn't care that this was happening. A leader who promised swift and decisive action to keep Muslims in their place had a ready audience.

RACISM

Lindsborg, Kansas, a small town 200 miles east of Garden City, prides itself on being a little Swedish community where visitors can purchase brightly painted dala horses and walk up the street to the Birger Sandzen memorial art gallery on the Bethany College campus. But on September 3, 2016, chalk graffiti appeared on several of the town's sidewalks declaring "Make Lindsborg White Again." Speculation ranged from suggestions that the message was inspired by Trump's "Make America Great Again" slogan to incredulity that a community already 97 percent white could prompt such racism. Perhaps, some suggested, it was merely a prank from a rival football team to embarrass the town. However, it did add to the national conversation about an upsurge of white nationalism.

In the days following the incident police determined that it was directed at the president of Bethany College, whose family included two adopted biracial children and whose campus included African American students. Anonymous phone calls to the president threatened him personally and said the "movement" was going to shut down the campus. The college and the community responded with public resolutions affirming their commitment to diversity.[6]

Further investigation revealed that the perpetrator was indeed a white nationalist, a nineteen-year-old from a nearby town who admitted to the incidents. The nationalist organization he and five or six others were associated with was a "white identitarian" network the Southern Poverty Law Center said believed the United States was "under assault by the forces of multiculturalism and political correctness."[7]

The incident was an example, just as the bombing plot in Garden City was, of bigotry surfacing in rural communities. It demonstrated that hate speech and hate crimes can and do happen anywhere. At the same time, it clearly deviated from the norm.

Racist attitudes toward African Americans among the larger population of white rural Americans are best summarized the way the Hispanic mayor of Garden City did—people don't come right out and say it, but there is a lot of prejudice. The implicit prejudice surfaced most often under the rubric of "riff-raff," which meant people on the margins of small towns who did not pull their weight, did not work hard or use their money responsibly, and expected something for nothing. Riff-raff could be anybody—white Anglo, Hispanic, or African American—but in communities where there were any African Americans, they were the implied referent. The trouble with riff-raff was not only that they did not fit in and did not seem personally responsible like others in the community. It was also that they were receiving special privileges from the government because of who they were.

Jeff Cahill in Gulfdale, where approximately 30 percent of the population was African American, was vehement in his opposition to entitlement programs, which he was sure the outsiders in his community were exploiting. "I don't mind helping people who are willing to help themselves," he said. "But just because you're over here or you're that color, or this or that, I don't think the government just owes you something because you know how to beat the system. I know a lot of minorities and they know how to work the system. They're riding around in expensive vehicles and I'm paying for their kids' lunch!"

People who Mr. Cahill's remarks would have made uncomfortable took what they considered a more progressive position on race relations. Their view was that race relations had been bad in the past but their communities had made enormous progress.

Marjorie Smith, a white municipal employee in a Deep South community of five thousand of whom a majority are African American, was one such person. "There are old-school people who are prejudiced on both sides, black and white," she says. "Some other communities in the area are still that way, where things are done for this group or that group," meaning segregated. But she insisted that wasn't true in her town. "Those kinds of changes just happen. I don't believe anybody can make them happen. They just do over time."

As evidence, she said there used to be two swimming pools in town, one for blacks and one for whites, but for some reason (lack of upkeep?) nobody swam in the black pool so the community filled it and turned it into a playground and now "we just have one pool and everybody can swim there. Slowly and surely those changes are happening."

African American community leaders acknowledged change, too, but with greater emphasis on the struggles involved and the barriers still in place. Plant closings hit the African Americans in their communities harder than the white workers who seemed to have more savings to fall back on. African Americans had to rely more on extended family members and on churches. White administrators of welfare programs found ways to discourage potential recipients. Gerrymandering and voter suppression were major obstacles to overcome.

Cedric Scott, the former mayor of Brooks Landing, a predominantly African American Delta community of three thousand, said the town had been devastated five years ago when the main manufacturing plant in town that employed five hundred people relocated. People who could find work elsewhere did, but many stayed and remained unemployed. The high school has a high dropout rate and Mr. Scott, who has a post-college degree, has resigned himself to the fact that kids with talent are likely to leave and the ones who stay are going to need menial jobs.

The barriers the community faces, Mr. Scott says, are institutional more than they are attitudinal. For example, when the plant closed it was hard for people to commute to jobs in other towns because there was no rural public transportation system. The state government hadn't considered it important. Without public transportation, it was difficult for people to get to the hospital, too; it was 30 miles away. Another barrier is that the community and surrounding area's population decline resulted in the loss of a congressional seat. The biggest positive change Mr. Scott can think of is that the town's economic development board is now racially mixed. Even that was a difficult transition, but it proved to be a blessing. With a diverse board, it could secure a couple of small grants that would not have been available otherwise.

The racism that many observers have wondered about is less about local affairs, though, than attitudes toward President Obama. Was some of the distrust of Washington racist? And was that among the reasons rural Americans voted the way they did in 2012 and again in 2016?

The people we talked to held nothing back in criticizing what they did not like about Obama. They called him a socialist, a raving liberal, somebody from a different planet, a president who did not know how to get anything done, and a person who made them physically sick. As one of the people we spoke with in a western state that nearly always went Republican by large margins said, "If I could speak to the President, I'd say 'Get off your bum, you doofus. Take care of things. Leave our Constitution alone!'" However, they rarely said anything that implied they did not like President Obama because of his race.

Stella Wright, a recently retired high school teacher in Gulfdale, was an exception. "I wish President Obama would just move to Australia," she said. "The present administration is the worst thing that's ever happened in this country!"

Pausing for breath, she continued, "I don't want anything bad to happen to him, but . . . I think he's terrible. I think history will prove he's the worst president we've ever had.

"And, and, I wish, I wish he wasn't black, because if he were white, everybody would realize this. But since he's black, people think that if you criticize him you're prejudiced."

She interrupted herself momentarily to explain that she and the people she knows are *not* prejudiced—"We have blacks in our church."

"But he, he's just a puppet. He's doing a terrible job!"

MISOGYNY

Had it not been that Hillary Clinton was the Democratic presidential candidate in 2016, the question of misogyny in rural America would likely never have come up. However, it is a question that merits serious attention. None of the men we interviewed said anything to the effect that women should not be in politics or the labor force or talked disparagingly about "the girls in the front office" or "the little woman in the kitchen."

It was rather that traditional gender roles were built into the social fabric of rural communities. Not that women stayed at home and did all the housework while the men in their lives were the breadwinners. It was more the fact that farm couples, for instance, divided the labor of running the farm in ways their parents had. The man drove the tractor, repaired the machinery, and fed the livestock; the woman ran errands, drove a truck during harvest, and did the bookkeeping. The division fell along the lines of who was assumed to be best suited for heavy manual labor. Yet, despite advances in technology that reduced much of the physical labor required, the roles remained the same. When one or both spouses also had a full- or part-time off-farm job, which was true in the clear majority of cases, it was usually the wife who had the longer commute.

Among townspeople, traditional gender roles manifested themselves in women being expected to do more of the housework and more of the childcare even when they held full-time jobs. Neighborly help, church work, and volunteering fell most heavily on their shoulders. And when there was an elderly parent or parent-in-law, women shouldered most of the responsibility for caregiving. "My husband and I would like to take a vacation some year," one of the women in Gulfdale told us, "but with both of us working and me taking care of Mama full time since she had her stroke five years ago, we just haven't gotten around to it."

Women we spoke with also acknowledged that it was difficult having planned on a career that required a college education, getting one, and then finding themselves living in a small town. They did not regret being married and having children, when that was the case, and they generally found reason to be upbeat about the comforts of rural life, but they admitted how discouraging it had been to give up their careers.

DIVERSITY

At this writing it remains to be seen whether the bigotry that surfaced during the 2016 presidential election and the white nationalism that gained so much interest will continue to be emboldened. It was certainly disheartening to those on the left who hoped America's growing ethnic, religious, and racial diversity was making us both stronger and more accepting. What we do know from years of research about prejudice and discrimination is that it is difficult to root out. Education usually helps and so does personal contact. But not always. Education is more effective when it includes active and extended teaching about the U.S. Constitution, which apparently is lacking, and contact fails to mitigate prejudice when people are only in a diverse context and make no efforts to know and respect people different from themselves. Lacking effective messaging against it, silent suppressed bigotry can easily be mobilized.

Most people living in rural America are probably no more prone toward bigotry than many people living in suburbs and cities. However, the small number who are willing to post "make America white" in chalk graffiti and the even smaller number willing to commit violent hate crimes are there just as they are in larger communities. Small-town police departments and county sheriffs already stretched thin may find it difficult to monitor such crimes.

The anger that prompts rural Americans to lash out at Washington is a source of bigotry as well. It can be a thin line from arguing that Washington is broken to saying that President Obama was illegal, stupid, and untrustworthy because he was African American. When communities feel threatened, they are not above reassuring themselves by seeking scapegoats.

Epilogue

When fake news, conspiracy theories, extremist rhetoric, foreign hacking, and questionable election results—when a large swath of the American population appears to have gone off the rails—it is difficult to take an objective perspective toward a part of the country that has by many accounts been complicit in that derangement. I'm part of the liberal elite. I teach at an Ivy League university and live in an upscale community that nearly always votes for Democrats. I support a woman's right to choose, marriage equality, and black lives matter. Over the years I've protested the Vietnam War, opposed nearly everything about the Reagan and Bush administrations, favored much of President Obama's efforts, and voted for Hillary Clinton.

This is my world. It feels right. So it is not easy to understand what feels equally right to people who live in communities radically different from mine. But as a researcher, that's what I've tried to do. I've deliberately sought out people whose views differ from mine. I've attempted to understand them as fairly and as objectively as I can.

I at least had a reference point. I went to grade school in a Kansas town of six hundred. The school has stood empty for decades. The Methodist church does what it can for struggling families. I went to high school in a town of five thousand that has dwindled to less than half that size. I was happy living there. It was home. People who currently make it their home still take pride in their community. But the ones I know feel left behind. They gave Trump 74 percent of their votes.

My message for fellow academics and "producers of knowledge" in the liberal elite is that rural America is not crazy. To be sure, they live in a world constructed by Rush Limbaugh and Fox News and Donald Trump. They overwhelmingly vote Republican, in many instances like they have for decades. Some of them participate in rallies where people scream invectives at Democrats and the media. Some of them publicly condone racial slurs and homophobia. Most of them do not. Their outrage is quieter. It remains hidden most of the time. It is built into the conversation at the coffee shop and the co-op. It surfaces at odd moments in candid interviews and sometimes with surprising vehemence.

The odd thing about most of the reportage interpreting rural America is that it has nothing to do with the communities in which rural Americans live. It's all about private resentments and personal attitudes. It's as if rural Americans spent their time in isolation pondering only their pocketbooks. Maybe it takes a sociologist to point out that rural Americans live in communities. It shouldn't. Towns are the best evidence we have that people do populate the vast reaches of rural America. Look around. Towns are everywhere.

Nor is it always the case that rural Americans live in small towns because they are stuck there and can't leave. That may be true of some of them, as we've seen, but it isn't the spirit in which most people talk about their community. They take pride in it. They usually care about it. The values they share with their neighbors seem right to them. This is the moral community that surrounds them.

A moral order is a hard thing to pin down. I've suggested that it is the collective, community-wide cultural reality in which people live. Its power in people's lives exists in the fact that it is taken for granted much of the time. You do not question what you do not see. Besides that, it works. The daily tasks of going from home to work and back, buying groceries, sending the kids to school, and greeting a neighbor are habits that require relatively little moment-to-moment deliberation. The conversation after church affirms an implicit agreement about the values you believe in and the public figures you respect. If you disagree, you keep your opinions to yourself.

When a moral order is threatened, the fact that it is usually taken for granted makes it difficult to identify exactly what the trouble is. You tell yourself your community is doing fine. It's a good place to live. It's had problems before and it's always come through. People are strong. The community is resilient. But it makes you mad that people elsewhere, especially in Washington, don't see it that way. They don't seem to behave responsibly like you do. They're devoid of common sense. They talk and talk but don't get anything constructive done. Their interests are with people who live in cities and don't look like you. They don't share your concern for the unborn and the sanctity of marriage. The ideas you associate with these interests, the ones that seem so different from your own, are powerful. They exist in privileged locations unlike yours. They threaten the way of life you want to preserve.

The line from these perceptions of threat to the political stage passes through the boundedness that separates the local community from the exterior world. Transgressions of the boundary dramatize the differences. The news from Washington that enters your living room via your television and your home computer on social media is astonishingly different from what you know among your family and friends. Research in fact demonstrates that it is often clearer to see what you disagree with than it is to specify what you yourself take for granted. The "us" and "them" distinction depends less on articulating what it is about "us" that we like than what we dislike about "them."

The further connection between threats and politics is that being afraid prompts us to *act*. This is the normal response. We are programmed to respond to fear by doing something. Often what we do is an immediate instinctive response. Often that response is wrong in retrospect and requires rethinking to get it right. Hitting someone we perceive as a threat or initiating a war when our country is attacked may not have been the best response in hindsight, but doing *something* made us feel stronger.

People who feel their rural communities are threatened have few options for taking action that will make them feel stronger. They are too law-abiding most of the time to join an armed militia and too nice to yell a racial slur at a Walmart clerk. The kind of action in their wheelhouse is listening faithfully to Rush Limbaugh and voting to shut down Planned Parenthood. It is invigorating to imagine kicking the government out of one's farm business and even more energizing to imagine draining the swamp in Washington.

In the same way that hitting someone is probably not the best response, relishing the idea of draining the swamp isn't likely to produce the desired results either. In my interviews, the most common response when asked about the federal government was simply to ridicule it and argue that voters should clean house or shut it down. When asked about specific policies, people knew that Social Security and Medicare were helping their communities. They conceded that subsidized crop insurance was probably a good thing. Some of them mentioned federal grants that assisted in building a new hospital or that provided emergency disaster relief. But these were not in the forefront of their minds.

Worrisome as it is for the vitality of American democracy, it is not surprising then that an election can be held in which hardly any discussion of concrete policies takes place. All that matters is outrage at the officeholders who the party you favor says should be thrown out of Washington. Clean the house. Drain the swamp. Whatever happens after that is too much to think about. Decisive action will have been taken.

Rural people of course are not unique in this regard. Suburbanites and city people are often angry about something the government has done too. Or they fear that the latest election spells doom. Rural people do however participate in the same society that all of us do—the one we all hope can work for our collective well-being.

While it is understandable that rural people think their communities are in danger and that their lifestyles are under siege, the truth from community leaders and ordinary citizens who live in these places suggests that outrage is not their only response. They may be driven by ideological appeals in national elections, but they are also pragmatic. When Washington seems unlikely to pay them much attention, no matter which party is in power, their pragmatism turns in other directions. It turns to local and regional solutions and to economic development projects, state government initiatives, and technological innovation. Pragmatism is as much about hope as it is about major accomplishments.

Where the best hope lies depends greatly on where it has been found in the past. Rural communities have long memories that fuel lasting loyalties. The chances of Democrats winning local elections in counties that have been Republican for generations are nil. But the chances of conservative Republicans being displaced by moderate Republicans—or vice versa—are high. And in many rural communities, Republicans' hold is not that strong.

Community leaders understand that fear and anger alone are not the key to their communities' survival. The town that gets the new hospital or small manufacturing facility is better off than the neighboring town that doesn't. And a state legislature's ruling majority must balance citizens' concerns about the quality of local schools and the availability of local healthcare against ideological appeals that have worked in the past.

Part of the moral fabric in rural communities is a kind of stubborn resilience. The same people who want Washington to get out of their lives also usually feel an obligation to stay put and try to make things turn around. Defending their values means more than lashing out or hunkering down. It also requires doing what they can to keep their communities vibrant. It necessitates meeting new challenges and adapting to changing conditions, even when the changes seem threatening.

NOTES

INTRODUCTION

1. Danielle Kurtzleben, "Rural Voters Played a Big Part in Helping Trump Defeat Clinton," *NPR*, November 14, 2016, www.npr.org; Lazaro Gamlo, "Urban and Rural America Are Becoming Increasingly Polarized," *Washington Post*, November 17, 2016, www.wp.com.
2. Rich Morin, "Behind Trump's Win in Rural White America," *Pew Research Center*, November 17, 2016, www.pewresearch.org.
3. Quoctrung Bui, "Actually, Income in Rural America Is Growing, Too," *New York Times*, September 16, 2016, www.nyt.com.
4. Charles M. Blow, "Trump's Rural White America," *New York Times*, November 14, 2016, www.nyt.com.
5. Dee Davis quoted in Helena Bottemiller Evich, "Revenge of the Rural Voter," *Politico*, November 13, 2016.
6. Ben Smith, "Obama on Small-town Pa.: Clinging to Religion, Guns, Xenophobia," *Politico*, April 11, 2008, www.politico.com.
7. U.S. Department of Agriculture, *Report on the Definition of "Rural."* Washington, DC: Government Printing Office, 2013.
8. My research assistants were Aislinn Addington, Bruce Carruthers, Phillip Connor, Janice Derstine, Emily Dumler, Justin Farrell, Brittany Hanstad, Sylvia Kundrats, Karenna Martin, Paul Martin, Christi Martone, Karen Myers, Steve Myers, Cynthia Reynolds, Shayne Runnion, Devany Schulz, Melissa Virts, and Lori Wiebold-Lippisch. They are the "we" to whom I make frequent reference in discussing the research. The interviews

included townspeople and farmers living in or near approximately three hundred small towns in forty-three states. The research results, including extensive material from the interviews and details about the interviews, are presented in my books, *Remaking the Heartland: Middle America Since the 1950s*; *Small-Town America: Finding Community, Shaping the Future*; and *In the Blood: Understanding America's Farm Families*.

9. Émile Durkheim, *The Elementary Forms of Religious Life*, trans. Karen E. Fields (New York: Free Press, 1995 [1912]).

10. Thorstein Veblen, "The Country Town," from *Absentee Ownership and Business Enterprise in Recent Times* (1923), ch. 7; *The Portable Veblen* (New York: Viking, 1948), 407.

1. COMMUNITIES

1. Mary Douglas, "The Idea of a Home: A Kind of Space," *Social Research* 58, 1 (1991), 287–307; quote on p. 303.

2. Fairfield and the other two towns introduced in this chapter as examples—Newborough and Gulfdale—are actual towns of the size and in the regions I indicated, but these are not the towns' real names, which protects the confidentiality of the persons interviewed in them. Actual town names are used for Lebanon, Smith Center, Garden City, Lindsborg, and Wichita; other town names are pseudonyms.

3. Pseudonyms are used throughout and some aspects of persons discussed (such as their official titles) are altered to disguise their identities. All the individuals discussed are real people with whom confidential interviews were conducted.

4. U.S. Census Bureau, "Our Changing Landscape," *Measuring America*, December 8, 2016, www.census.gov.

5. Robert Wuthnow, *Small-town America Finding Community, Shaping the Future* (Princeton, NJ: Princeton University Press, 2013), 54.

6. Benedict Anderson, *Imagined Communities: Reflections on the Origin and Spread of Nationalism* (New York: Verso, 1983), 6.
7. Wuthnow, *Small-town America*, 18–19, 48; U.S. Census Bureau, 2010, residents of incorporated places and New England towns; household income data drawn from the merged 2005 to 2009 American Community Surveys, http://www.socialexplorer.com.
8. Randall Collins, *Interaction Ritual Chains* (Princeton, NJ: Princeton University Press, 2005).
9. This summary is based on Suzanne Keller, *Community: Pursuing the Dream, Living the Reality* (Princeton, NJ: Princeton University Press, 2003).

2. PRESENT DANGERS

1. Wuthnow, *Small-town America*, 396–97.
2. Mark Baechtel, "Dead Center America," *Washington Post*, January 16, 2000.
3. Robert Wuthnow, *Remaking the Heartland: Middle America since the 1950s* (Princeton, NJ: Princeton University Press, 2011), 7–20.
4. Robert J. Sampson, "Neighborhood and Community: Collective Efficacy and Community Safety," *New Economy* 11 (2004), 106–13.
5. W. F. Cottrell, "Death by Dieselization: A Case Study in the Reaction to Technological Change," *American Sociological Review* 16, 3 (1951), 358–65.
6. Robert Wuthnow, *In the Blood: Understanding America's Farm Families* (Princeton, NJ: Princeton University Press, 2015).
7. Wuthnow, *Small-town America*, 81–83.
8. Patrick J. Carr and Maria J. Kefalas, *Hollowing Out the Middle: The Rural Brain Drain and What It Means for America* (Boston: Beacon Press, 2009).

9. Camille L. Ryan and Julie Siebens, "Education Attainment in the United States: 2009," *Current Population Reports*, February 2012.

10. Émile Durkheim, *Suicide* (New York: Free Press, 1951 [1897]).

11. Laura Moser, "Another Year, Another Anti-Evolution Bill in Oklahoma," *Slate*, January 25, 2016.

12. "Teen Birthrate Is Higher in Small U.S. Towns than in Cities," *Washington Post*, November 18, 2016.

13. Wuthnow, *Small-town America*, 444.

14. Haeyoun Park and Matthew Bloch, "How the Epidemic of Drug Overdose Deaths Ripples Across America," *New York Times*, January 19, 2016.

15. I was the principal investigator on this study, the main results of which are included in Robert Wuthnow, *Loose Connections: Joining Together in America's Fragmented Communities* (Cambridge, MA: Harvard University Press, 1998); the dataset is available online at www.thearda.com.

3. MAKESHIFT SOLUTIONS

1. Alexis de Tocqueville, *Democracy in America*, ed. J. P. Mayer, trans. George Lawrence (New York: Harper Perennial, 1966 [1835]).

2. Robert D. Putnam, *Bowling Alone: The Collapse and Revival of American Community* (New York: Simon & Schuster, 2000), 2005.

3. Wuthnow, *Loose Connections*, 135–38, 233–37.

4. Wuthnow, *Small-town America*, 179–83.

5. Terrence McCoy, "Disabled, or Just Desperate? Rural Americans Turn to Disability as Jobs Dry Up," *Washington Post*, March 30, 2017.

6. Wuthnow, *In the Blood*.

7. Kirsten Tretbar, *Zenith* (Shawnee Mission, KS: Prairie Fire Films, 2001).

4. WASHINGTON'S BROKEN

1. H. L. Mencken, "On Law Enforcement," *Chicago Daily Tribune*, December 11, 1927; Richard Hofstadter, "The Paranoid Style in American Politics," *Harper's Magazine* (November 1964); reprinted in *The Paranoid Style in American Politics, and Other Essays* (New York: Vintage, 2008); and referenced as context for the 2016 presidential election in Thomas B. Edsall, "The Paranoid Style in American Politics Is Back," *New York Times*, September 8, 2016, and Conor Lynch, "Paranoid Politics: Donald Trump's Style Perfectly Embodies the Theories of Renowned Historian," *Salon*, July 7, 2016.
2. Wuthnow, *Small-town America*, 313–18; Theda Skocpol and Vanessa Williamson, *The Tea Party and the Remaking of Republican Conservatism* (New York: Oxford University Press, 2012); Arlie Russell Hochschild, *Strangers in Their Own Land: Anger and Mourning on the American Right* (New York: New Press, 2016).
3. Robert Wuthnow, *Rough Country: How Texas Became America's Most Powerful Bible-belt State* (Princeton, NJ: Princeton University Press, 2014), 432–47.
4. David E. Campbell and Robert D. Putnam, "Crashing the Tea Party," *New York Times*, August 16, 2011.

5. MORAL DECLINE

1. Wuthnow, *Small-town America*, 269, 436.
2. Details of the events from 1975 leading to the Tiller murder in 2009 are provided in Robert Wuthnow, *Red State Religion: Faith and Politics in America's Heartland* (Princeton, NJ: Princeton University Press, 2012), 287–303, 326–30.
3. Wuthnow, *Small-town America*, 279, 437.
4. Ibid.

5. Larry M. Bartels, "What's the Matter with *What's the Matter with Kansas?*" *Quarterly Journal of Political Science* 1 (2006), 201–26.
6. Michele Dillon and Sarah Savage, "Values and Religion in Rural America: Attitudes toward Abortion and Same-Sex Relations," *Carsey Institute Issue Brief* 1 (Fall 2006), 1–10.

6. BIGOTRY

1. David Paul Kuhn, "Sorry, Liberals. Bigotry Didn't Elect Donald Trump," *New York Times*, December 26, 2016.
2. Wuthnow, *Small-town America*, 92–94.
3. These results are from further analysis of the 2003 Diversity Survey, which I designed and conducted; both the survey results and information from qualitative interviews are present in Robert Wuthnow, *America and the Challenges of Religious Diversity* (Princeton, NJ: Princeton University Press, 2005).
4. A. G. Sulzberger, "Hispanics Reviving Faded Towns on the Plains," *New York Times*, November 13, 2011.
5. Robert Wuthnow, *American Mythos: Why Our Best Efforts to Be a Better Nation Fall Short* (Princeton, NJ: Princeton University Pres, 2006).
6. Kristine Guerra, "'Make Lindsborg White Again': Racist Messages Target College President with Biracial Children," *Washington Post*, September 22, 2016.
7. Andy Marso, "Young White Nationalist Seeks Foothold in Kansas Politics," *Kansas Health Service News Service*, September 28, 2016, www.khl.org/news.

FURTHER READING

OVERVIEWS OF RURAL AMERICA

Adamy, Janet and Paul Overberg. "Rural America Is the New 'Inner City.'" *Wall Street Journal*, May 26, 2017.

Brown, David L. and Kai A. Schafft. *Rural People and Communities in the 21st Century*. Malden, MA: Polity Press, 2011.

Brown, David L. and Louis E. Swanson, editors. *Challenges for Rural America in the Twenty-First Century*. University Park: Pennsylvania State University Press, 2003.

Flora, Cornelia Butler, Jan L. Flora, and Stephen P. Gasteyer. *Rural Communities: Legacy and Change*. Boulder, CO: Westview Press, 2016.

United States Department of Agriculture. "Rural America at a Glance." *Economic Information Bulletin* (November 2016), 1–6.

Wood, Richard. *Survival of Rural America: Small Victories and Bitter Harvests*. Lawrence: University Press of Kansas, 2008.

Wuthnow, Robert. *Remaking the Heartland: Middle America Since the 1950s*. Princeton, NJ: Princeton University Press, 2011.

Wuthnow, Robert. *Small-Town America: Finding Community, Shaping the Future*. Princeton, NJ: Princeton University Press, 2013.

HISTORICAL BACKGROUND

Danbom, David B. *Born in the Country: A History of Rural America*, 2nd ed. Baltimore: Johns Hopkins University Press, 2006.

Douglass, H. Paul. *The Little Town: Especially in Its Rural Relationships*. New York: Macmillan, 1919.

Dykstra, Robert R. "Town-Country Conflict: A Hidden Dimension in American Social History." *Agricultural History* 38 (1964), 195–204.

Egan, Timothy. *The Worst Hard Time*. New York: Houghton Mifflin, 2006.

Goodwyn, Lawrence. *The Populist Moment: A Short History of the Agrarian Revolt in America*. New York: Oxford University Press, 1978.

Lingeman, Richard. *Small Town America: A Narrative History, 1620–The Present*. New York: Putnam, 1980.

Riney-Kehrberg, Pamela, ed. *The Routledge History of Rural America*. New York: Routledge, 2016.

Vidich, Arthur J. and Joseph Bensman. *Small Town in Mass Society: Class, Power, and Religion in a Rural Community*. Princeton, NJ: Princeton University Press, 1958.

West, James. *Plainville, U.S.A.* New York: Columbia University Press, 1945.

DEMOGRAPHY

Albrecht, Don E. "Nonmetropolitan Population Trends: Twenty-First Century Updates." *Journal of Rural Social Sciences* 25 (2010), 1–21.

Artz, Georgeanne M. and Peter F. Orazem. "Reexamining Rural Decline: How Changing Rural Classifications Affect Perceived Growth." *Review of Regional Studies* 36 (2006), 163–91.

Chi, Guangqing. "The Impacts of Highway Expansion on Population Change: An Integrated Spatial Approach." *Rural Sociology* 75 (2010), 58–89.

Fuguitt, Glenn V. "County Seat Status as a Factor in Small Town Growth and Decline." *Social Forces* 44 (1965), 245–51.

Fuguitt, Glenn V., David L. Brown, and Calvin L. Beale. *Rural and Small Town America*. New York: Russell Sage Foundation, 1989.

Semuels, Alana. "The Graying of Rural America." *Atlantic*, June 2, 2016; available online at www.theatlantic.com.

COMMUNITY

Anderson, Benedict. *Imagined Communities: Reflections on the Origin and Spread of Nationalism*. London: Verso, 1991.

Bender, Thomas. *Community and Social Change in America*. Baltimore: Johns Hopkins University Press, 1978.

Ehrenhalt, Alan. *The Lost City: The Forgotten Virtues of Community in America*. New York: Basic Books, 1995.

Fischer, Claude S. *To Dwell Among Friends: Personal Networks in Town and City*. Chicago: University of Chicago Press, 1982.

Hummon, David M. "Popular Images of the American Small Town." *Landscape* 24 (1980), 3–9.

Hummon, David M. *Commonplaces: Community Ideology and Identity in American Culture*. New York: State University of New York Press, 1990.

Keller, Suzanne. *Community: Pursuing the Dream, Living the Reality*. Princeton, NJ: Princeton University Press, 2003.

McMillan, David W. and David M. Chavis. "Sense of Community: A Definition and Theory." *Journal of Community Psychology* 14 (1986), 6–23.

Salamon, Sonya. "From Hometown to Nontown: Rural Community Effects of Suburbanization." *Rural Sociology* 68 (2003), 1–24.

Salamon, Sonya. *Newcomers to Old Towns: Suburbanization of the Heartland*. Chicago: University of Chicago Press, 2003.

Sundblad, Daniel R. and Stephen G. Sapp. "The Persistence of Neighboring as a Determinant of Community Attachment:

A Community Field Perspective." *Rural Sociology* 76 (2011), 511–34.

Wuthnow, Robert. *Loose Connections: Joining Together in America's Fragmented Communities*. Cambridge, MA: Harvard University Press, 1998.

FARMS AND FARMERS

Beach, Sarah S. "'Tractorettes' or Partners? Farmers' Views on Women in Kansas Farming Households." *Rural Sociology* 78 (2013), 210–28.

Gardner, Bruce L. *American Agriculture in the Twentieth Century: How It Flourished and What It Cost*. Cambridge, MA: Harvard University Press, 2002.

Gill, Fiona. "Moving to the 'Big' House: Power and Accommodation in Inter-Generational Farming Families." *Rural Society* 18 (2008), 83–94.

Harlin, J. L. "The Aging Family Farm—Estate/Succession Planning for Farmers." *Agricultural Finance* 34 (1992), 38–39.

Hutson, John. "Fathers and Sons: Family Farms, Family Businesses and the Farming Industry." *Sociology* 21 (1987), 215–29.

Inwood, Shoshanah, Jill K. Clark, and Molly Bean. "The Differing Values of Multigeneration and First-Generation Farmers: Their Influence on the Structure of Agriculture at the Rural-Urban Interface." *Rural Sociology* 78 (2013), 346–70.

Lobao, Linda and Katherine Meyer. "The Great Agricultural Transition: Crisis, Change, and Social Consequences of Twentieth-Century US Farming." *Annual Review of Sociology* 27 (2001), 103–24.

Riney-Kehrberg, Pamela. *Childhood on the Farm: Work, Play, and Coming of Age in the Midwest*. Lawrence: University Press of Kansas, 2005.

Salamon, Sonya. *Prairie Patrimony: Family, Farming, and Community in the Midwest*. Chapel Hill: University of North Carolina Press, 1992.

Salamon, Sonya and Jane B. Tornatore. "Territory Contested through Property in a Midwestern Post-Agricultural Community." *Rural Sociology* 59 (1994), 636–54.

Tickamyer, Ann R. and Debra A. Henderson. "Rural Women: New Roles for the New Century?" In *Challenges for Rural America in the Twenty-First Century*, edited by David L. Brown and Louis E. Swanson, 109–17. University Park: Pennsylvania State University Press, 2003.

Wuthnow, Robert. *In the Blood: Understanding America's Farm Families*. Princeton, NJ: Princeton University Press, 2015.

RURAL CULTURE

Bell, Michael Mayerfeld. *Childerley: Nature and Morality in a Country Village*. Chicago: University of Chicago Press, 1994.

Bell, Michael Mayerfeld. "The Ghosts of Place." *Theory and Society* 26 (1997), 813–36.

Besser, Terry L., Nicholas Recker, and Kerry Agnitsch. "The Impact of Economic Shocks on Quality of Life and Social Capital in Small Towns." *Rural Sociology* 73 (2008), 580–604.

Bloom, Stephen G. *Postville: A Clash of Cultures in Heartland America*. New York: Mariner Books, 2001.

Boyles, Denis. *Superior, Nebraska: The Common Sense Values of America's Heartland*. New York: Doubleday, 2008.

Bryson, Bill. *The Lost Continent: Travels in Small-Town America*. New York: Harper Perennial, 1990.

Campbell, Hugh, Michael Mayerfeld Bell, and Margaret Finney, editors. *Country Boys: Masculinity and Rural Life*. University Park: Pennsylvania State University Press, 2006.

Ching, Barbara and Gerald W. Creed, editors. *Knowing Your Place: Rural Identity and Cultural Hierarchy*. New York: Routledge, 1997.

Curry, Janel M. "Community Worldview and Rural Systems: A Study of Five Communities in Iowa." *Annals of the Association of American Geographers* 90 (2000), 693–712.

Davies, Richard O., Joseph A. Amato, and David R. Pichaske, editors. *A Place Called Home: Writings on the Midwestern Small Town*. St. Paul: Minnesota Historical Society, 2003.

Douglas, Mary. "The Idea of a Home: A Kind of Space." In *Home: A Place in the World*, edited by Arien Mack, 253–72. New York: New York University Press, 1993.

Klinkenborg, Verlyn. *The Rural Life*. Boston: Little Brown, 2002.

Lavenda, Robert H. *Corn Fests and Water Carnivals: Celebrating Community in Minnesota*. Washington, DC: Smithsonian Institution Press, 1997.

Levy, Emanuel. *Small-Town America in Film: The Decline and Fall of Community*. New York: Continuum, 1991.

MacGregor, Lyn C. *Habits of the Heartland: Small-Town Life in Modern America*. Ithaca, NY: Cornell University Press, 2010.

McConnell, Eileen Diaz and Faranak Miraftab. "Sundown Town to 'Little Mexico': Old-timers and Newcomers in an American Small Town." *Rural Sociology* 74 (2009), 605–29.

Mueller, William. "Do Americans Really Want to Live in Small Towns?" *American Demographics* (January 1987), 34–37, 60.

Oldenburg, Ray. *The Great Good Place: Cafes, Coffee Shops, Community Centers, Beauty Parlors, General Stores, Bars, Hangouts, and How They Get You Through the Day*. New York: Paragon House, 1989.

RURAL MEMOIRS

Andersen, M. J. *Portable Prairie: Confessions of an Unsettled Midwesterner*. New York: Thomas Dunne, 2004.

Anderson, Leslie O. *Memoirs of a Country Boy / Newspaper Man*. Elk River, MN: DeForest Press, 2004.

Barnett, Bob. *Growing Up in the Last Small Town*. Ashland, KY: Jesse Stuart Foundation, 2010.

Beardslee, Bob. *Hometown Memories*. Victoria, BC: Trafford Publishing, 2006.

Bodensteiner, Carol. *Growing Up Country: Memories of an Iowa Farm Girl*. Des Moines, IA: Sun Rising Press, 2008.

Fowler, Eric B. and Sheila Delaney. *Small-Town Boy, Small-Town Girl: Growing Up in South Dakota, 1920–1950*. Pierre: South Dakota Historical Society, 2009.

Marquart, Debra. *The Horizontal World: Growing Up Wild in the Middle of Nowhere*. New York: Counterpoint, 2006.

Schwieder, Dorothy Hubbard. *Growing Up with the Town: Family and Community on the Great Plains*. Iowa City: University of Iowa Press, 2002.

Vance, J. D. *Hillbilly Elegy: A Memoir of a Family and Culture in Crisis*. New York: Harper Collins, 2016.

SOCIAL PROBLEMS

Anderson, Scott Thomas. *Shadow People: How Meth-driven Crime Is Eating at the Heart of Rural America*. New York: Coalition for Investigative Journalism, 2012.

Carr, Patrick J. and Maria J. Kefalas. *Hollowing Out the Middle: The Rural Brain Drain and What It Means for America*. Boston: Beacon, 2009.

Davidson, Osha Gray. *Broken Heartland: The Rise of America's Rural Ghetto*. Iowa City: University of Iowa Press, 1996.

Davies, Richard O. *Main Street Blues: The Decline of Small-Town America*. Columbus: Ohio State University Press, 1998.

Douthat, Ross. "The Roots of White Anxiety." *New York Times*, July 18, 2010.

Duncan, Cynthia M. *World Apart: Poverty and Politics in Rural America*, 2nd ed. New Haven, CT: Yale University Press, 2014.

Erikson, Kai T. *Everything in Its Path: Destruction of Community in the Buffalo Creek Flood*. New York: Simon & Schuster, 1977.

Glasmeier, Amy and Priscilla Salant. "Low-Skill Workers in Rural America Face Permanent Job Loss." *Carsey Research* (Spring 2006), 1–7.

Grey, Mark, Michele Devlin, and Aaron Goldsmith. *Postville U.S.A.: Surviving Diversity in Small-Town America*. Boston: Gemma Media, 2009.

Lichter, Daniel T., Domenico Parisi, Steven Michael Grice, and Michael C. Taquino. "National Estimates of Racial Segregation in Rural and Small-Town America." *Demography* 44 (2007), 563–81.

Loewen, James W. *Sundown Towns: A Hidden Dimension of American Racism*. New York: New Press, 2005.

Reding, Nick. *Methland: The Death and Life of an American Small Town*. New York: Bloomsbury, 2009.

Schaefer, Andrew, Marybeth J. Mattingly, and Kenneth M. Johnson. "Child Poverty Higher and More Persistent in Rural America." *Carsey Research* (Winter 2016), 1–7.

Schwartz-Barcott, Timothy Philip. *After the Disaster: Re-creating Community and Well-Being at Buffalo Creek since the Notorious Coal-Mining Disaster in 1972*. Amherst, NY: Cambria Press, 2008.

Sherman, Jennifer. "Coping with Rural Poverty: Economic Survival and Moral Capital in Rural America." *Social Forces* 85 (2006), 891–913.

Sherman, Jennifer. *Those Who Work, Those Who Don't: Poverty, Morality, and Family in Rural America*. Minneapolis: University of Minnesota Press, 2009.

Van Gundy, Karen. "Substance Abuse in Rural and Small Town America." *Carsey Institute Report on Rural America* 1 (2006), 5–36.

Weisheit, Ralph A., David N. Falcone, and L. Edward Wells. *Crime and Policing in Rural and Small-Town America*, 3rd ed. Long Grove, IL: Waveland Press, 2006.

ORGANIZATIONS

Bradshaw, Ted K. "Multicommunity Networks: A Rural Transition." *Annals of the American Academy of Political and Social Science* 529 (1993), 164–75.

Ford, Kristina, James Lopach, and Dennis O'Donnell. *Planning in Small Town America: Observations, Sketches, and a Reform Proposal.* Chicago: American Planning Association, 1990.

Hanna, Kevin S., Ann Dale, and Chris Ling. "Social Capital and Quality of Place: Reflections on Growth and Change in a Small Town." *Local Environment* 14 (2009), 31–44.

Landon, Donald D. *Country Lawyers: The Impact of Context on Professional Practice.* New York: Praeger, 1990.

Miller, Carol D. *Niagara Falling: Globalization in a Small Town.* Lanham, MD: Lexington Books, 2007.

Putnam, Robert D. *Bowling Alone: The Collapse and Revival of American Community.* New York: Simon & Schuster, 2000.

Rotolo, Thomas. "Town Heterogeneity and Affiliation: A Multilevel Analysis of Voluntary Association Membership." *Sociological Perspectives* 43 (2000), 272–89.

Tolbert, Charles M., Michael D. Irwin, Thomas A. Lyson, and Alfred R. Nucci. "Civic Community in Small-Town America: How Civic Welfare Is Influenced by Local Capitalism and Civic Engagement." *Rural Sociology* 67 (2002), 90–113.

POLITICS

Armey, Dick and Matt Kibbe. *Give Us Liberty: A Tea Party Manifesto.* New York: William Morrow, 2010.

Cramer, Katherine J. *The Politics of Resentment: Rural Consciousness in Wisconsin and the Rise of Scott Walker.* Chicago: University of Chicago Press, 2016.

Farah, Joseph. *The Tea Party Manifesto.* New York: WND Books, 2010.

Formisano, Ron. "Populist Currents in the 2008 Presidential Campaign." *Journal of Policy History* 22 (2010), 237–55.

Hochschild, Arlie Russell. *Strangers in Their Own Land: Anger and Mourning on the American Right.* New York: New Press, 2016.

Langer, Andrew M. "Sarah Palin, Small-Town America." *U.S. News*, September 12, 2008.

Leonard, Robert. "Why Rural America Voted for Trump." *New York Times*, January 5, 2017.

McKee, Seth C. "Rural Voters in Presidential Elections." *Forum* 5, 2 (2007), 1–24.

Peterson, Trudy. "Rural Life and the Privacy of Political Association." *Agricultural History* 64 (1990), 1–8.

Skocpol, Theda and Vanessa Williamson. *The Tea Party and the Remaking of Republican Conservatism.* New York: Oxford University Press, 2012.

Wuthnow, Robert. *Red State Religion: Faith and Politics in America's Heartland.* Princeton, NJ: Princeton University Press, 2012.

Wuthnow, Robert. *Rough Country: How Texas Became America's Most Powerful Bible-belt State.* Princeton, NJ: Princeton University Press, 2014.

SOCIAL ISSUES

Cohen, David S. and Krysten Cannon. *Living in the Crosshairs: The Untold Stories of Anti-Abortion Terrorism.* New York: Oxford University Press, 2015.

Dillon, Michele and Sarah Savage. "Values and Religion in Rural America: Attitudes Toward Abortion and Same-Sex Relations." *Carsey Institute Reports* (Fall 2006), 1–10.

Fellows, Will. *Farm Boys: Lives of Gay Men from the Rural Midwest.* Madison: University of Wisconsin Press, 2001.

Gray, Mary L. *Out in the Country: Youth, Media, and Queer Visibility in Rural America.* New York: NYU Press, 2009.

Gray, Mary L., Colin R. Johnson, and Brian J. Gilley, eds. *Queering the Countryside: New Frontiers in Rural Queer Studies*. New York: NYU Press, 2016.

Munson, Ziad W. *The Making of Pro-Life Activists: How Social Movement Mobilization Works*. Chicago: University of Chicago Press, 2009.

Thomson-Deveaux, Amelia. "Last Rural Abortion Clinics in Texas Shut Down." *American Prospect*, March 6, 2014.

IMMIGRATION

Albarracin, Julia. *At the Core and in the Margins: Incorporation of Mexican Immigrants in Two Rural Midwestern Communities*. East Lansing: Michigan State University Press, 2016.

Artz, Georgeanne M., Peter F. Orazem, and Daniel M. Otto. "Meat Packing and Processing Facilities in the Non-Metropolitan Midwest: Blessing or Curse?" Unpublished paper presented at the Annual Meeting of the American Agricultural Economics Association, Providence, Rhode Island, July 2005.

Artz, Georgeanne M., Peter F. Orazem, and Daniel M. Otto. "Measuring the Impact of Meat Packing and Processing Facilities in Nonmetropolitan Counties: A Difference-in-Differences Approach." *American Journal of Agricultural Economics* 89 (2007), 557–70.

Jensen, Leif. "New Immigrant Settlements in Rural America: Problems, Prospects, and Policies." *Carsey Institute Reports on Rural America* 1 (2006), 6–32.

Jimenez, Tomas R. "Mexican-Immigrant Replenishment and the Continuing Significance of Ethnicity and Race." *American Journal of Sociology* 113 (2008): 1527–67.

Jimenez, Tomas R. *Replenished Ethnicity: Mexican Americans, Immigration, and Identity*. Berkeley and Los Angeles: University of California Press, 2009.

Partridge, Mark D., Dan S. Rickman, and Kamar Ali. "Recent Immigration and Economic Outcomes in Rural America." *American Journal of Agricultural Economics* 90 (2008), 1326–33.

Ribas, Vanesa. *On the Line: Slaughterhouse Lives and the Making of the New South.* Berkeley and Los Angeles: University of California Press, 2016.

Stull, Donald D. and Michael J. Broadway. *Slaughterhouse Blues: The Meat and Poultry Industry in North America.* San Francisco: Wadsworth, 2004.

Waldorf, Brigitte S., Raymond J.G.M. Florax, and Julia Beckhusen. "Spatial Sorting of Immigrants Across Urban and Rural Areas in the United States: Changing Patterns of Human Capital Accumulation Since the 1990s." *American Journal of Agricultural Economics* 90 (2008), 1312–18.

Wuthnow, Robert. *America and the Challenges of Religious Diversity.* Princeton, NJ: Princeton University Press, 2005.

Wuthnow, Robert. *American Mythos: Why Our Best Efforts to Be a Better Nation Fall Short.* Princeton, NJ: Princeton University Press, 2006.

INDEX

abortion, 10, 63–64, 95, 122–29, 137–40, 161; adoption as alternative to, 64, 126; denominational differences on, 127–29; murder of Dr. George Tiller, 123, 125; personal responsibility and, 128; pro-choice position toward, 126–29, 138; pro-life networks and political mobilization, 114; rural opposition to, 123; as symptom of moral decline, 122

African Americans: gerrymandering and vote suppression, 140, 154; as portion of rural population, 143; racial segregation, 10–11, 37, 68; rural racism and, 2, 10, 151–56

agriculture: corporate agribusiness, 84, 99, 104, 143–44; as declining profession, 50–51; family farms, 15, 19–22, 51, 58, 75–76, 120; farmers as community leaders, 102–3; federal agricultural policy, 51, 84, 95, 99, 102–4; generational conflicts and family farms, 75–76; immigrant labor and, 37–38, 143–47; negative stereotypes of farmers, 58–59; political representation for small farmers, 84; rural economic decline and,

50–52; and small towns, 50–51; state and regional organizations and, 84; technology and changes in, 51–52, 75; unpredictability of income from, 92, 94

"altruistic suicide," 60
American Family Association, 114
Anderson, Alex, 72–74
Anderson, Benedict, 32
anger. *See* moral outrage
Ankerholz, Sheila, 135
assimilation into rural communities, 29–30, 147–48
athletic events, 14, 18, 41, 49, 121, 133

bigotry: anti-immigrant, 37–38, 141, 148; and hate crimes, 141–42, 150, 152, 158; misogyny, 156–57; moral outrage and, 142, 158; negative stereotypes of farmers, 58–59; politics and, 142, 148; race and rural, 10–11 (*see also* racism); religious, 149–51; remedies for, 157–58; stereotypes of rural Americans, 3, 28, 58–59, 73, 78, 94, 97–99, 112–13; white nationalism, 142, 150–52, 158